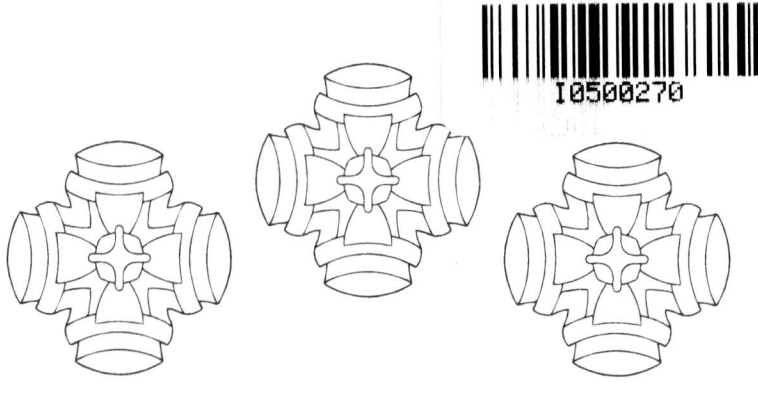

POCKET
PATTERNS

Lori's Pocket Pattern Coloring Books for Adults

VOLUME 1

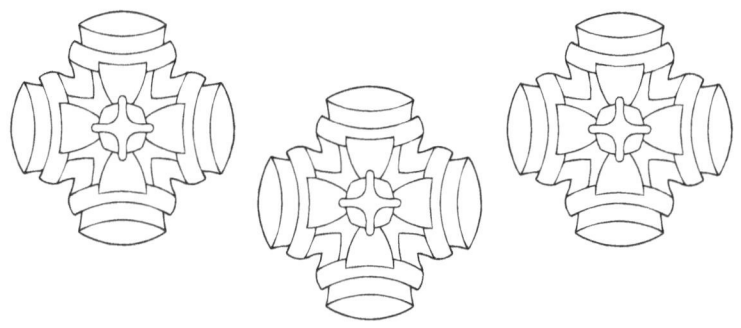

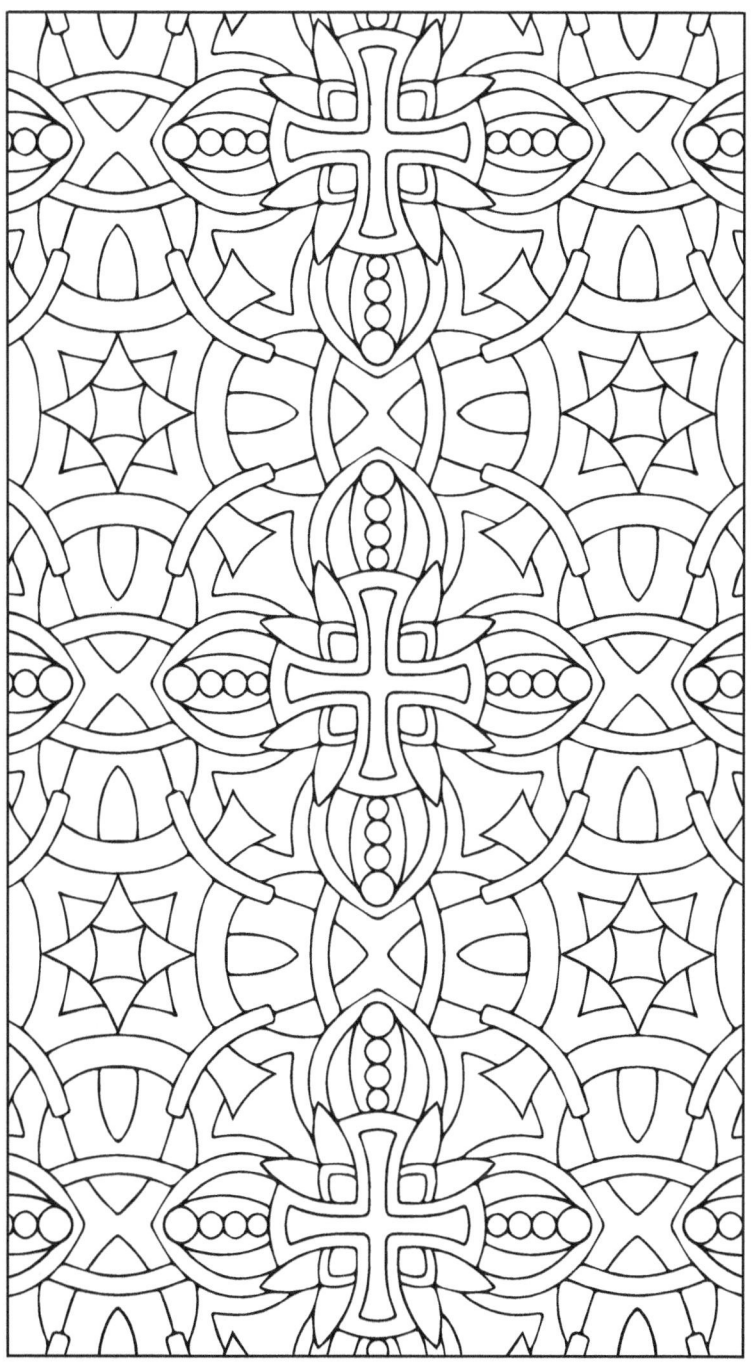

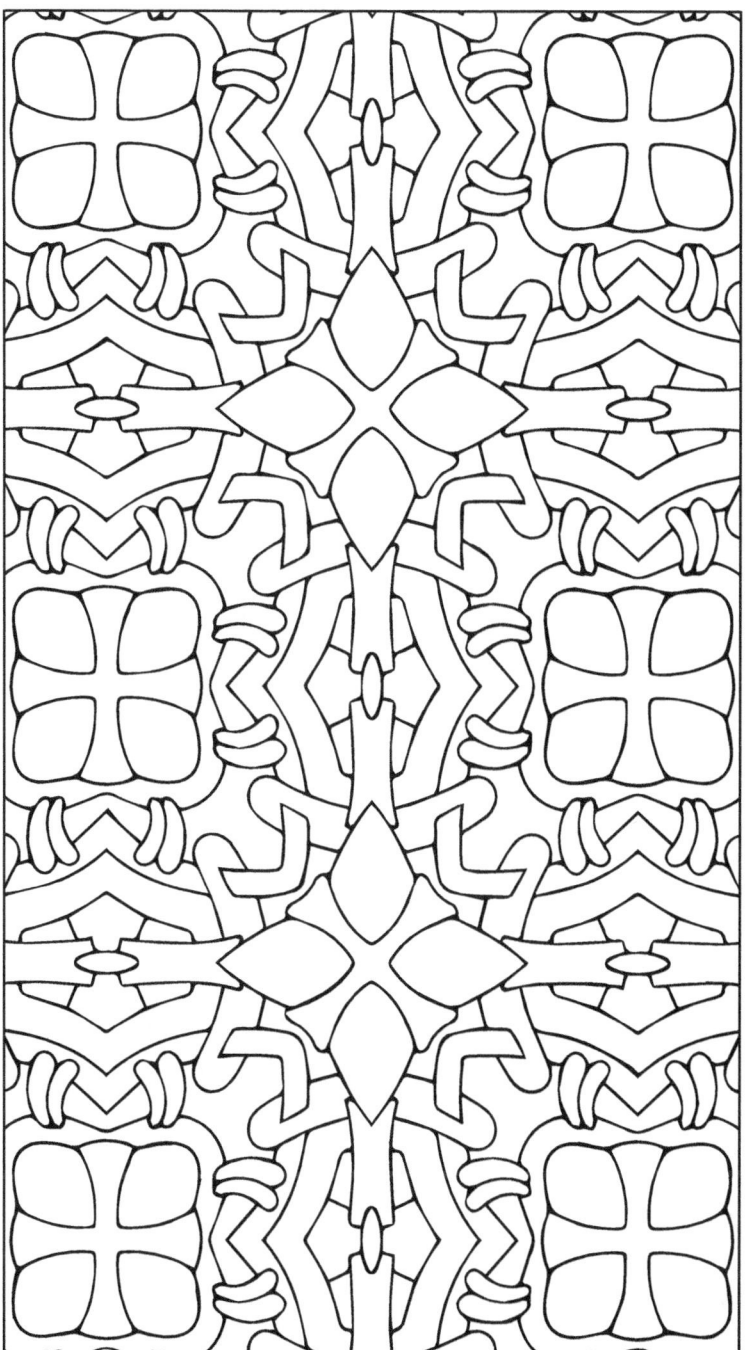

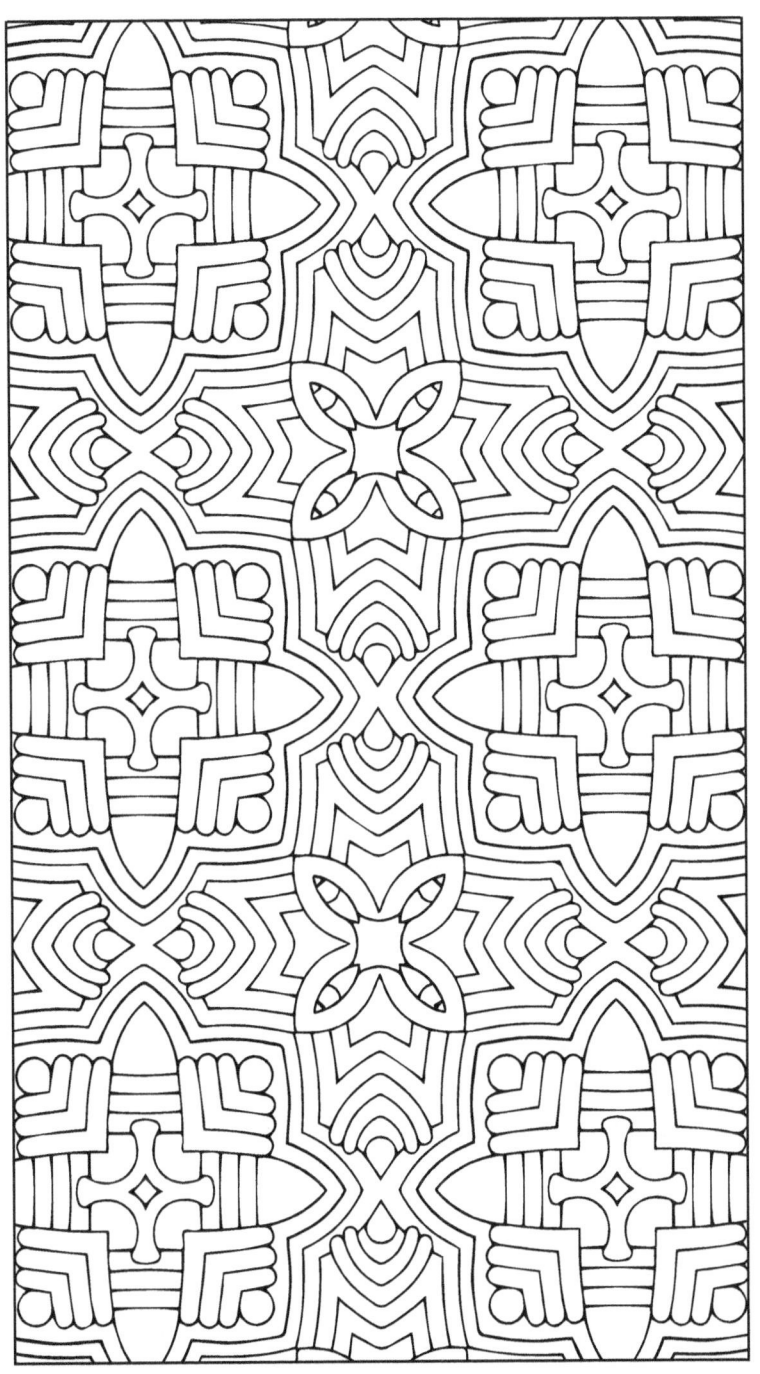

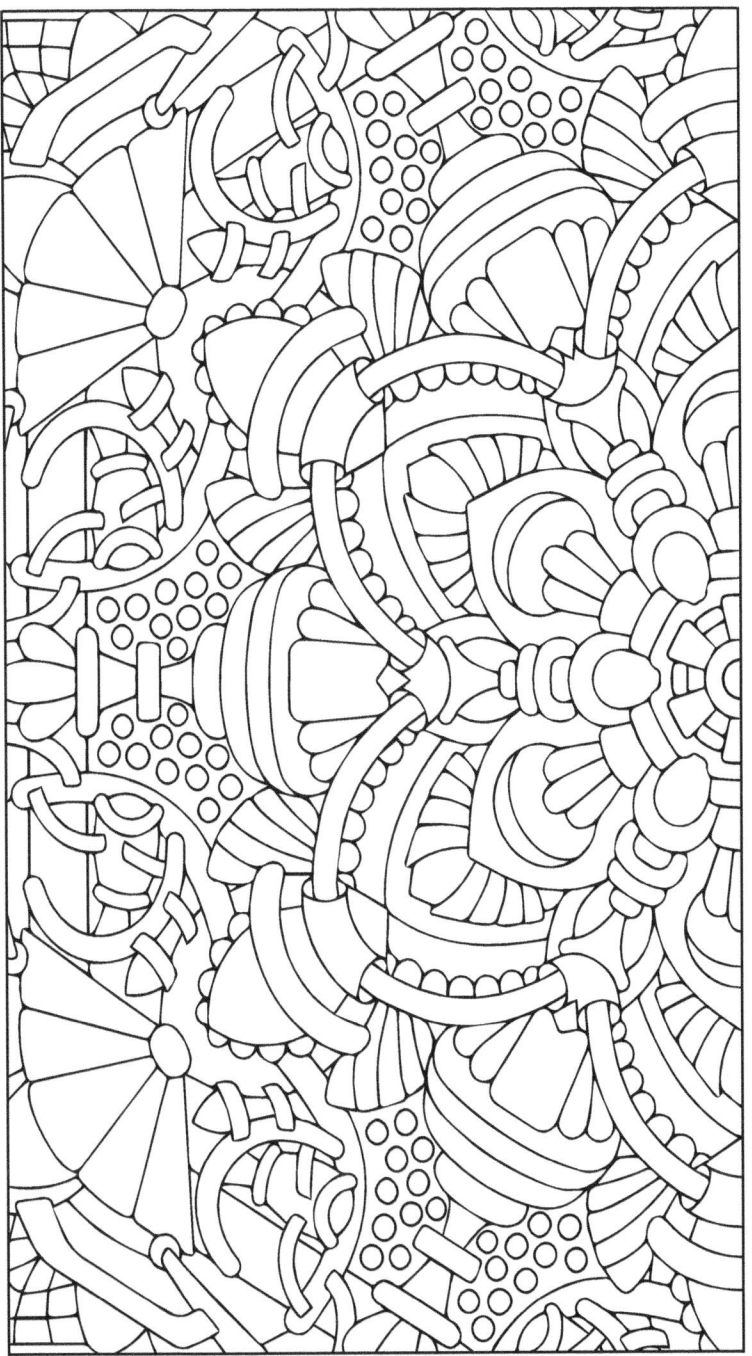

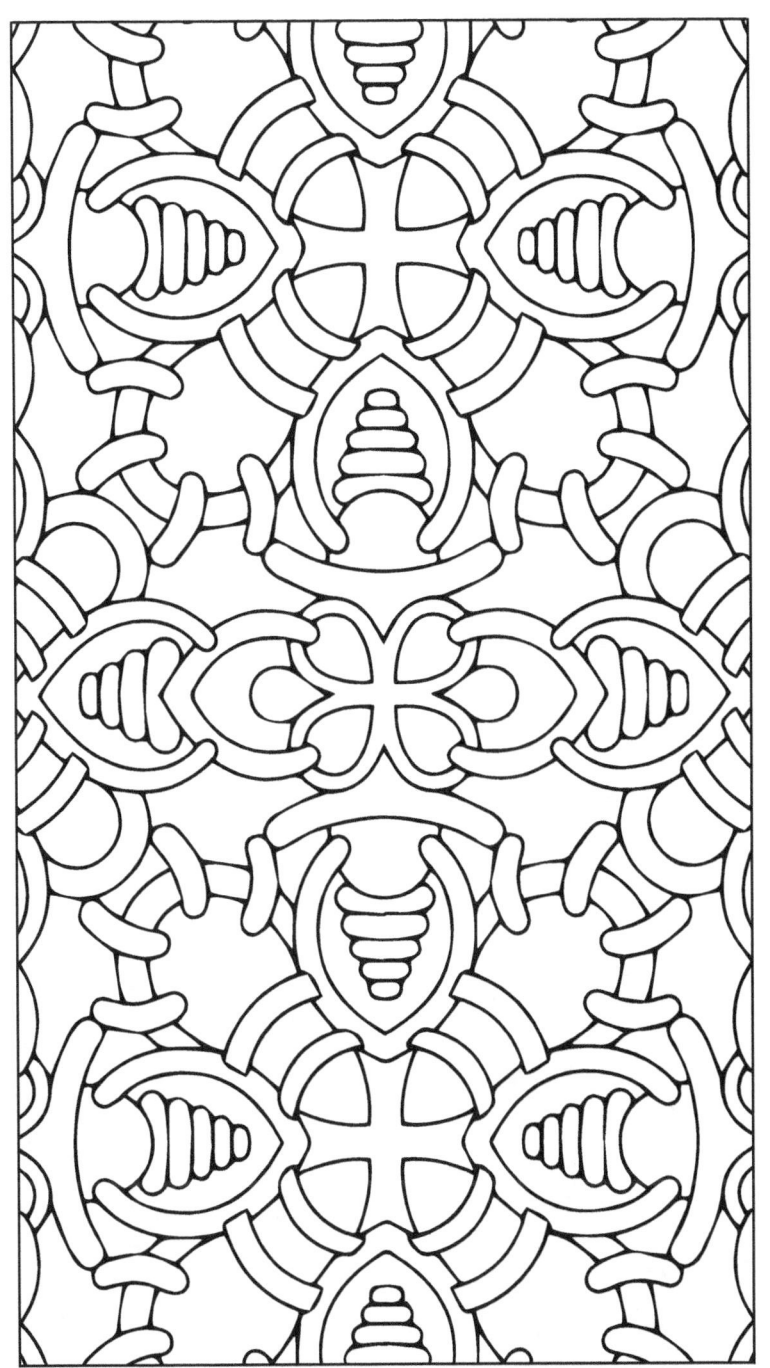

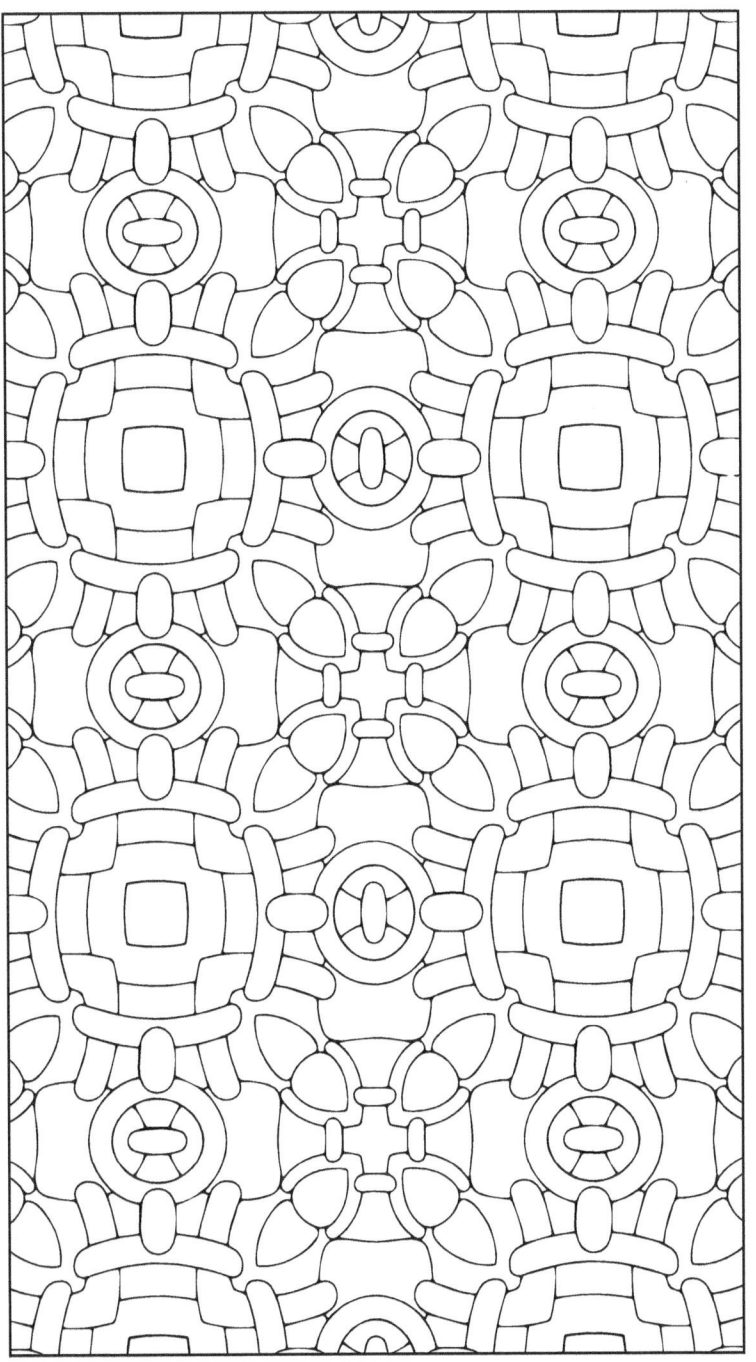

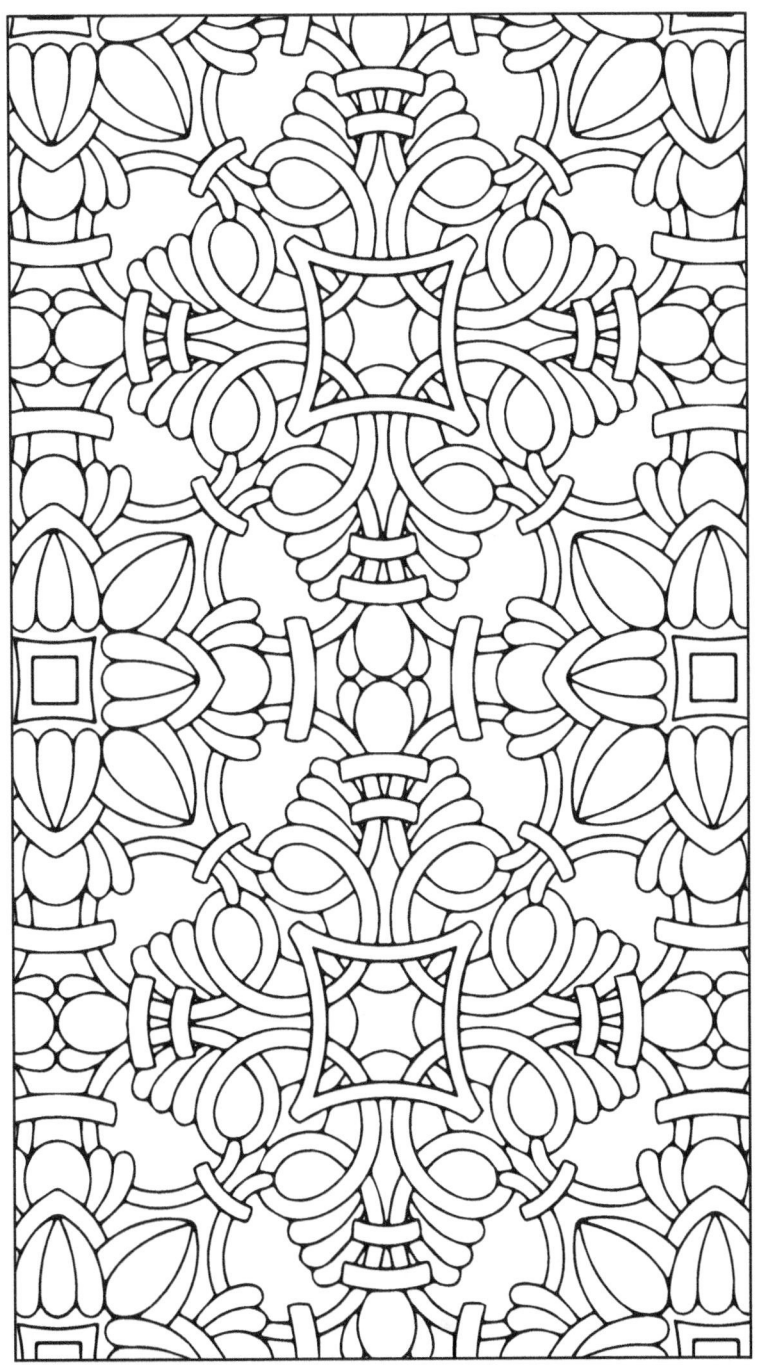

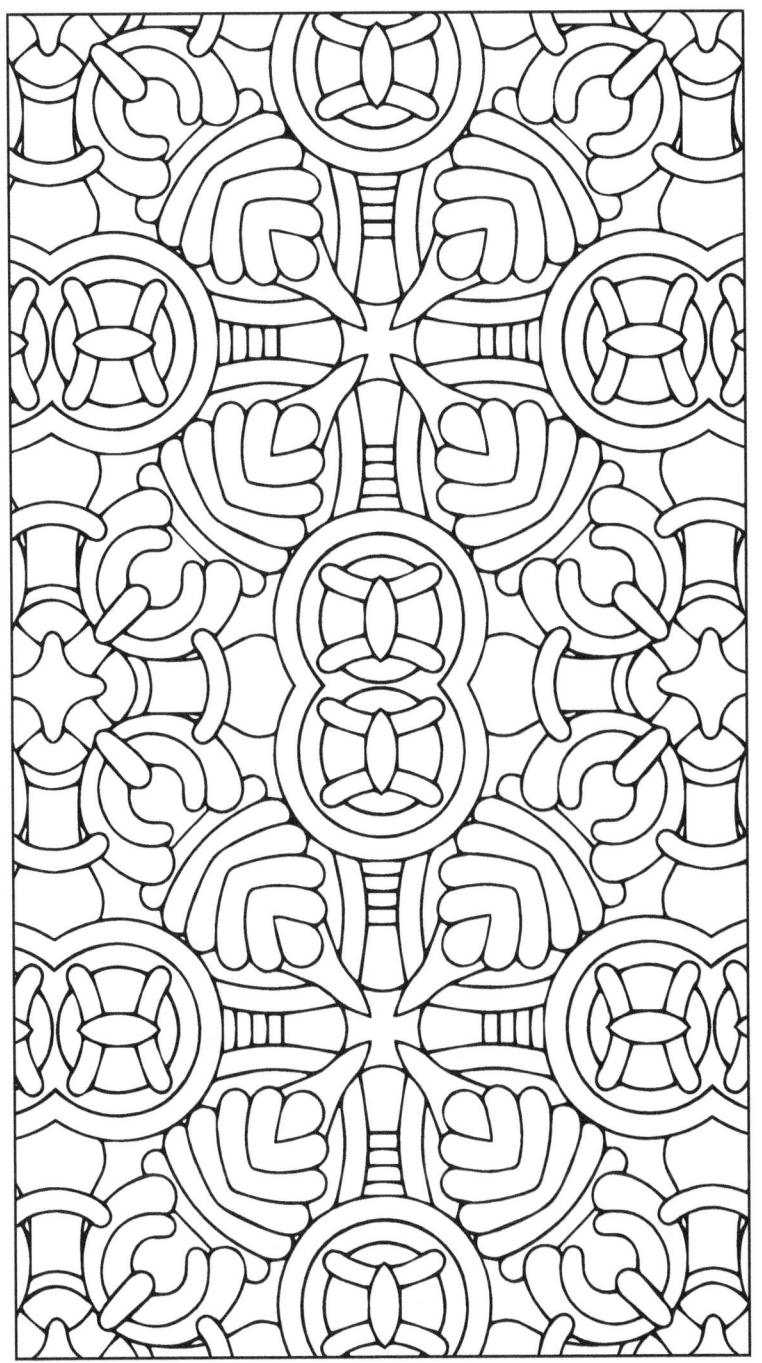

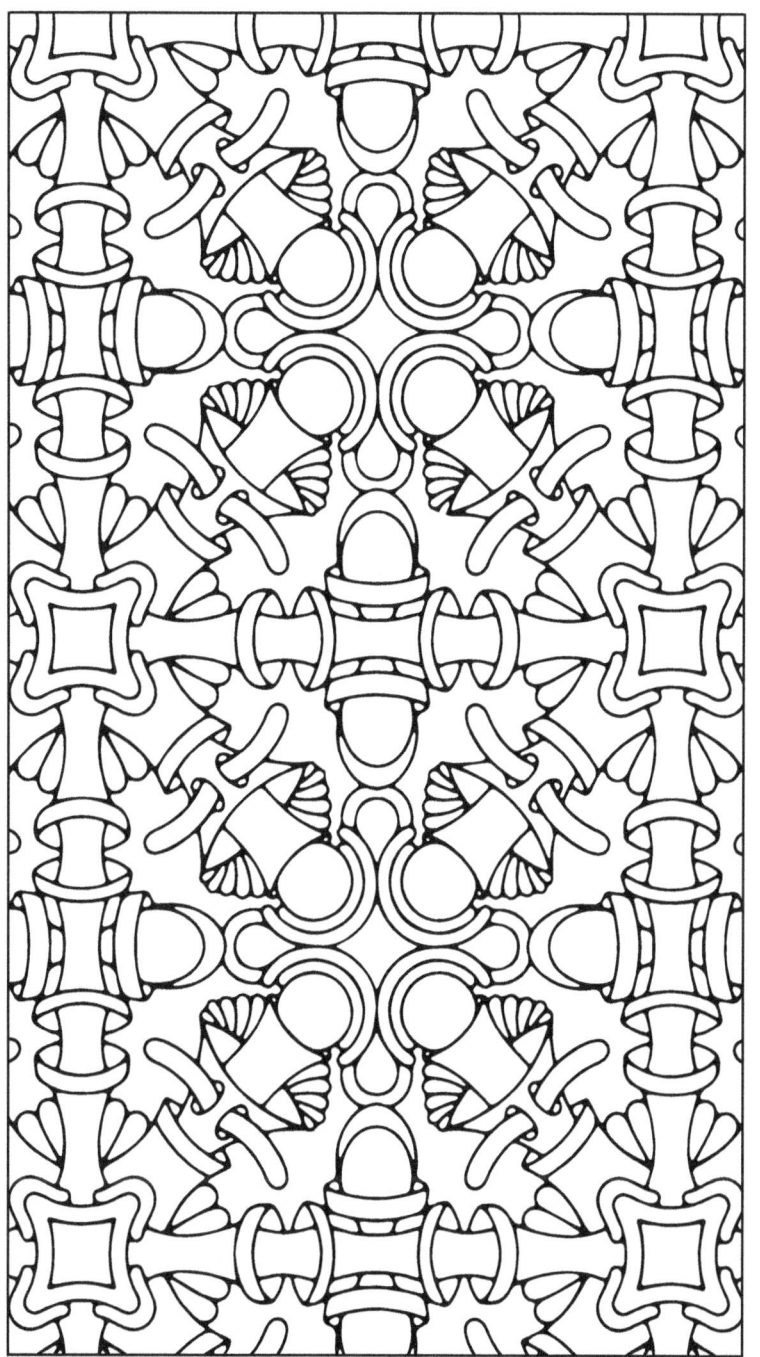

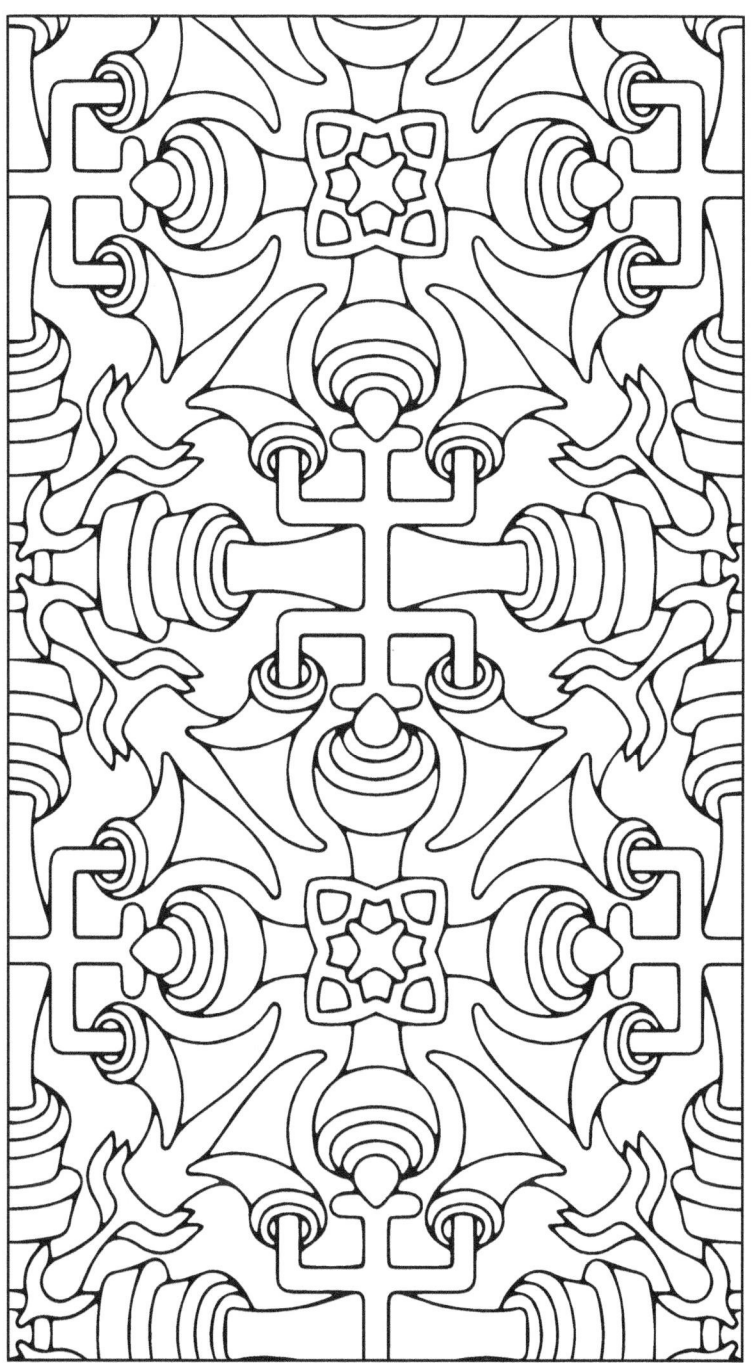

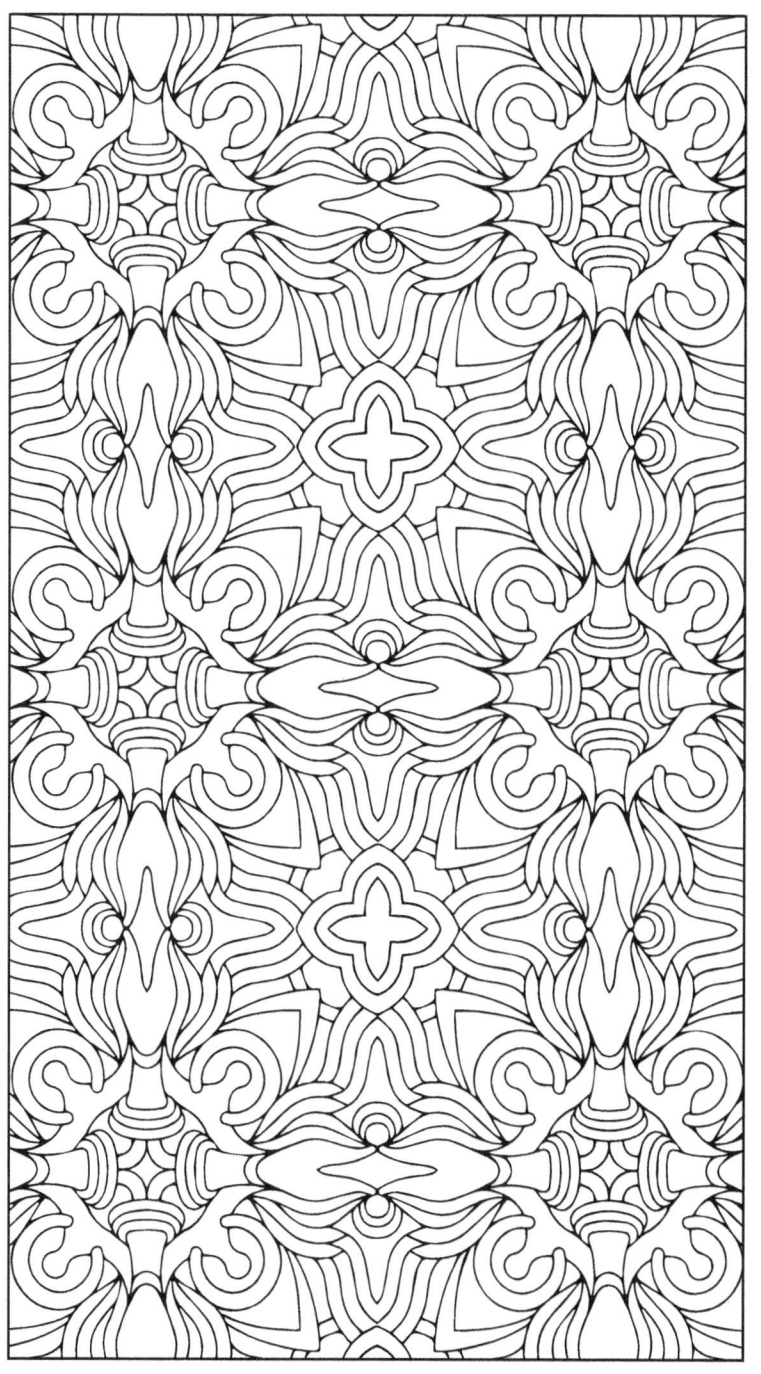

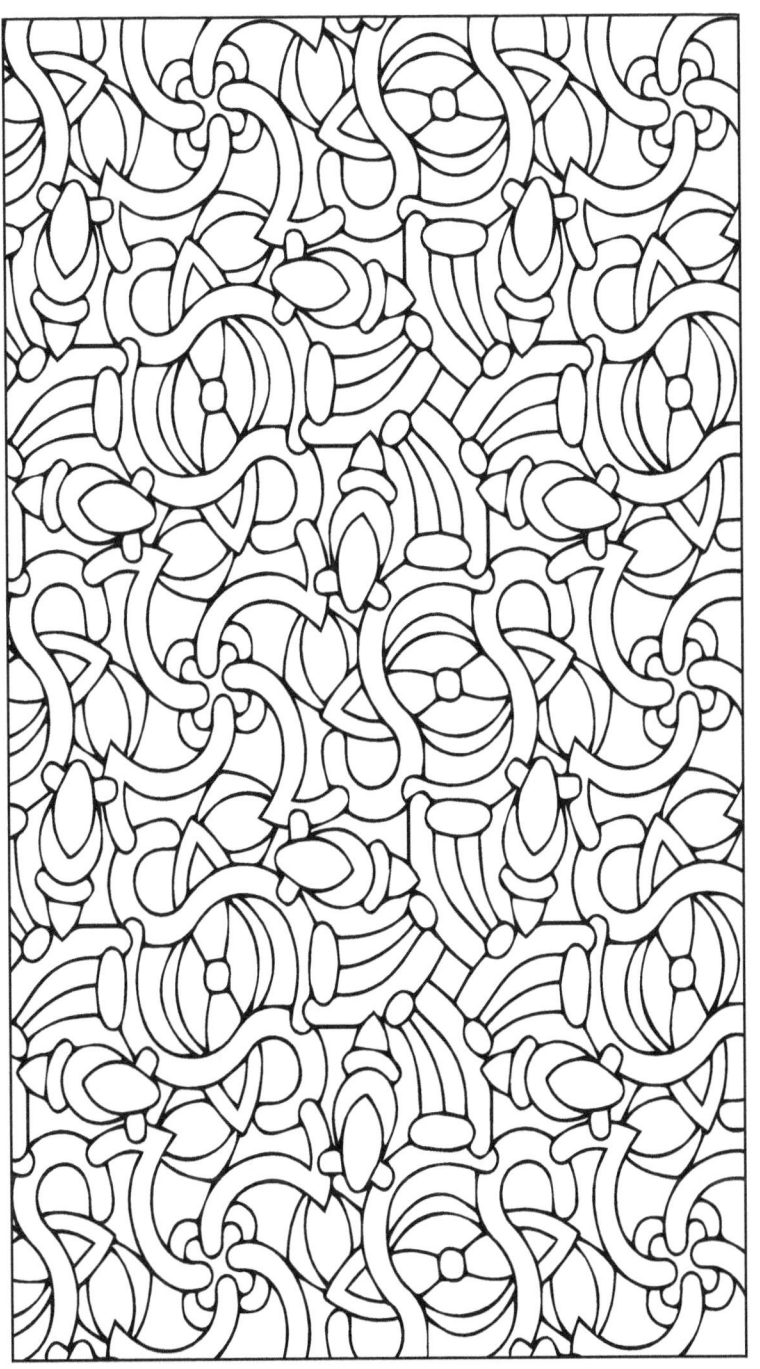

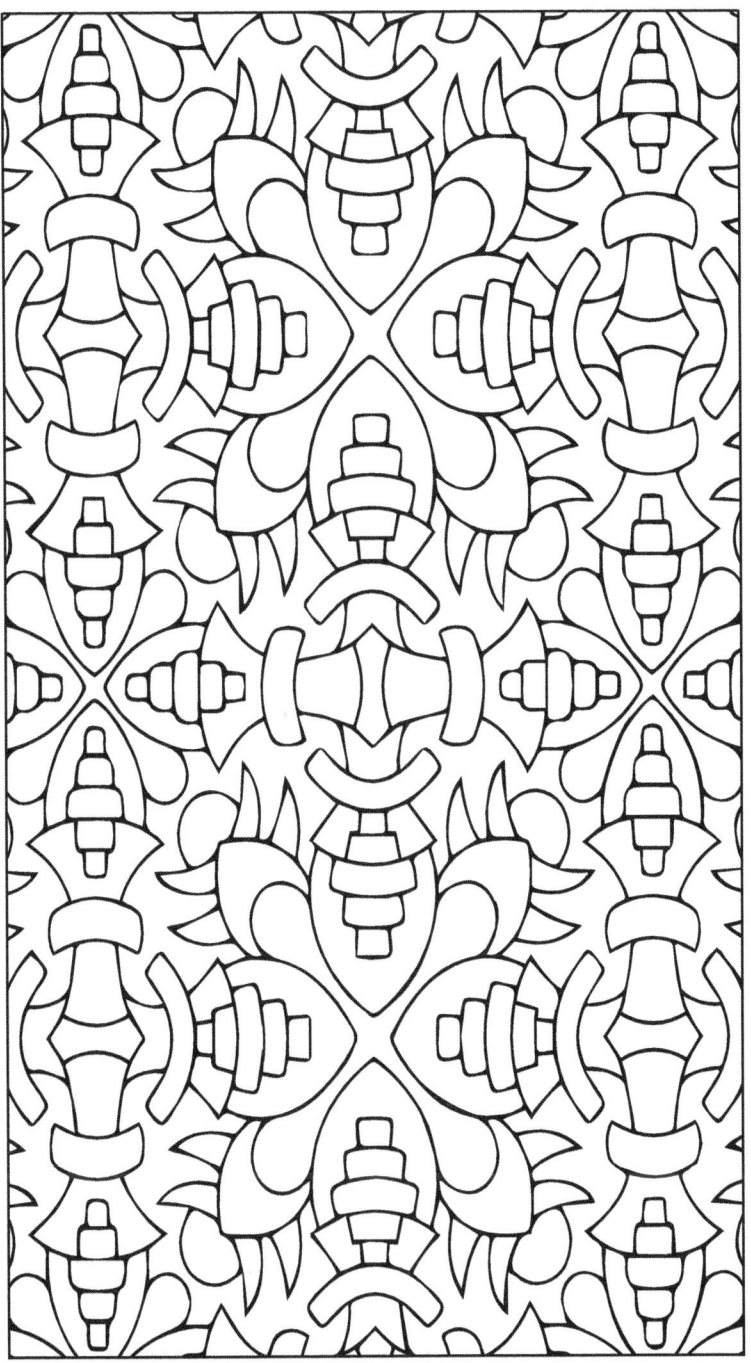

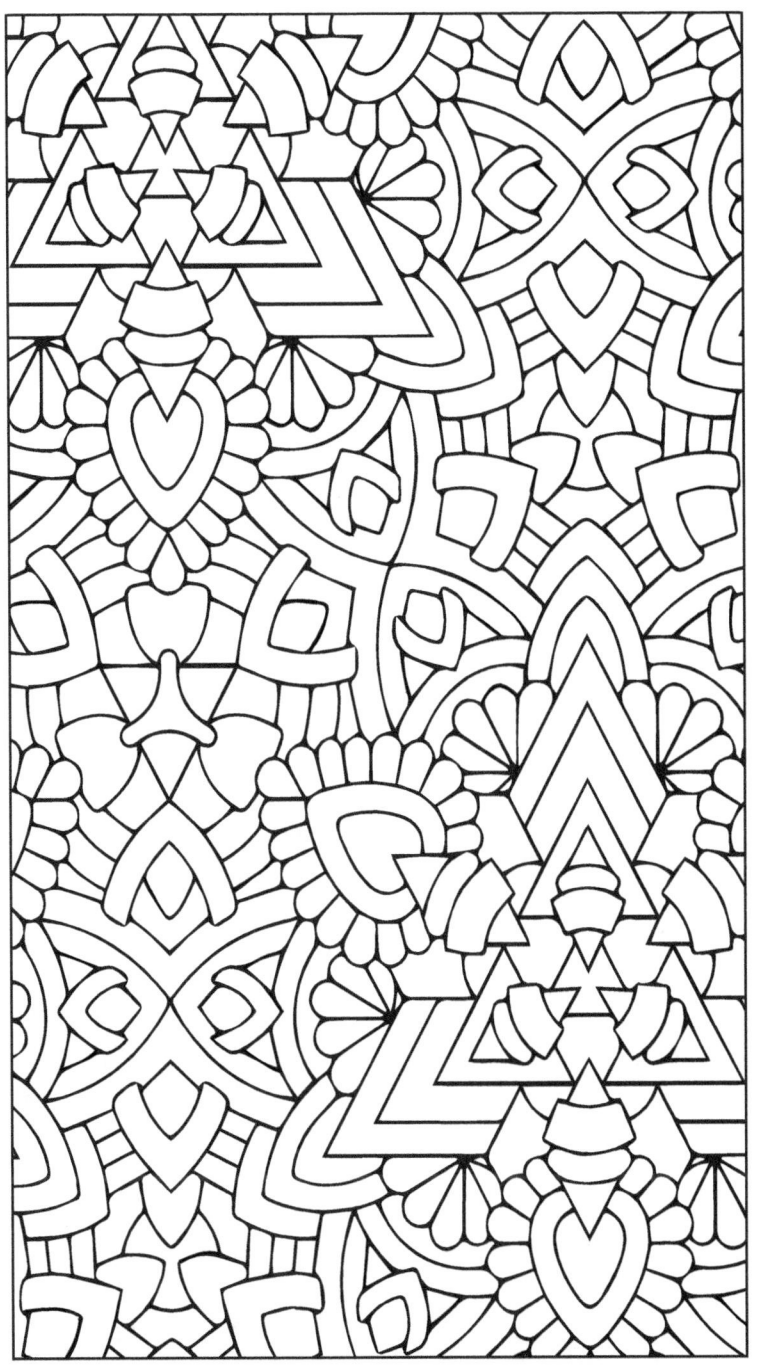

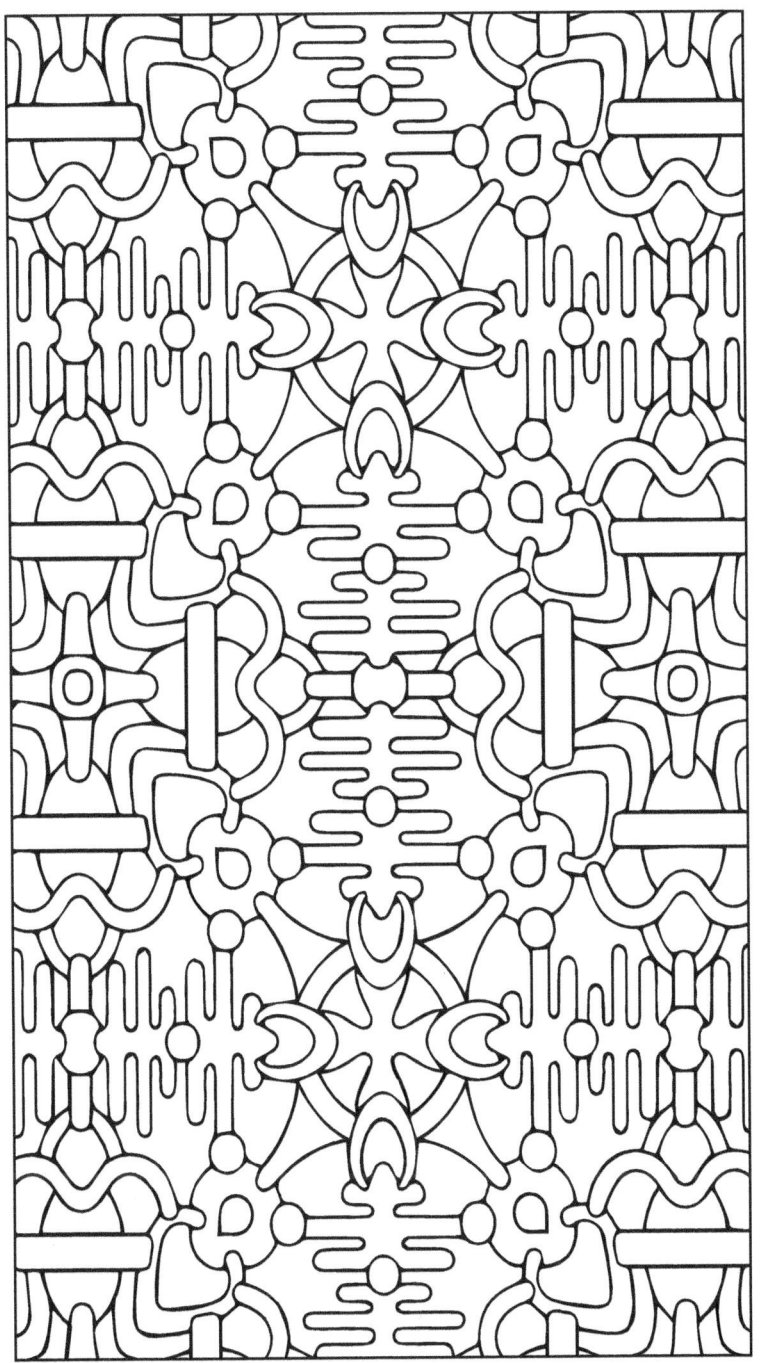

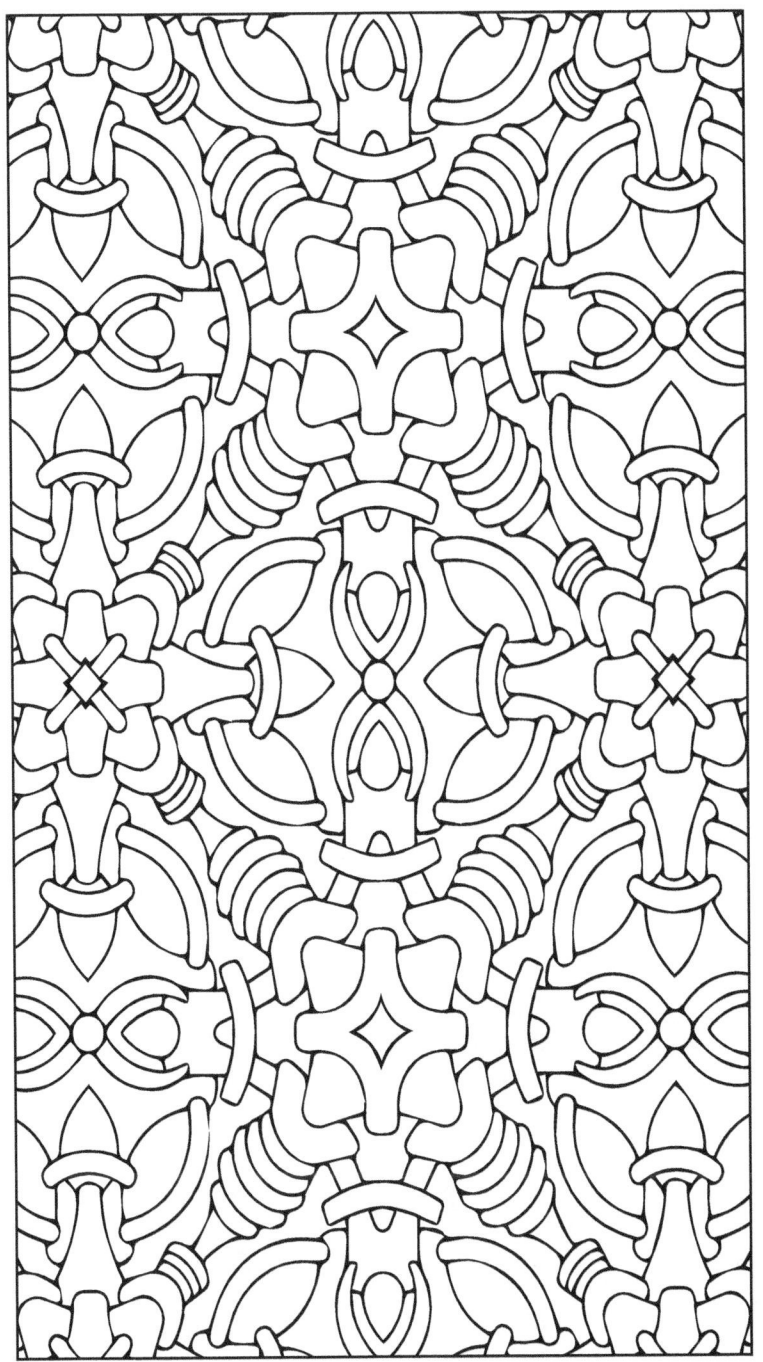

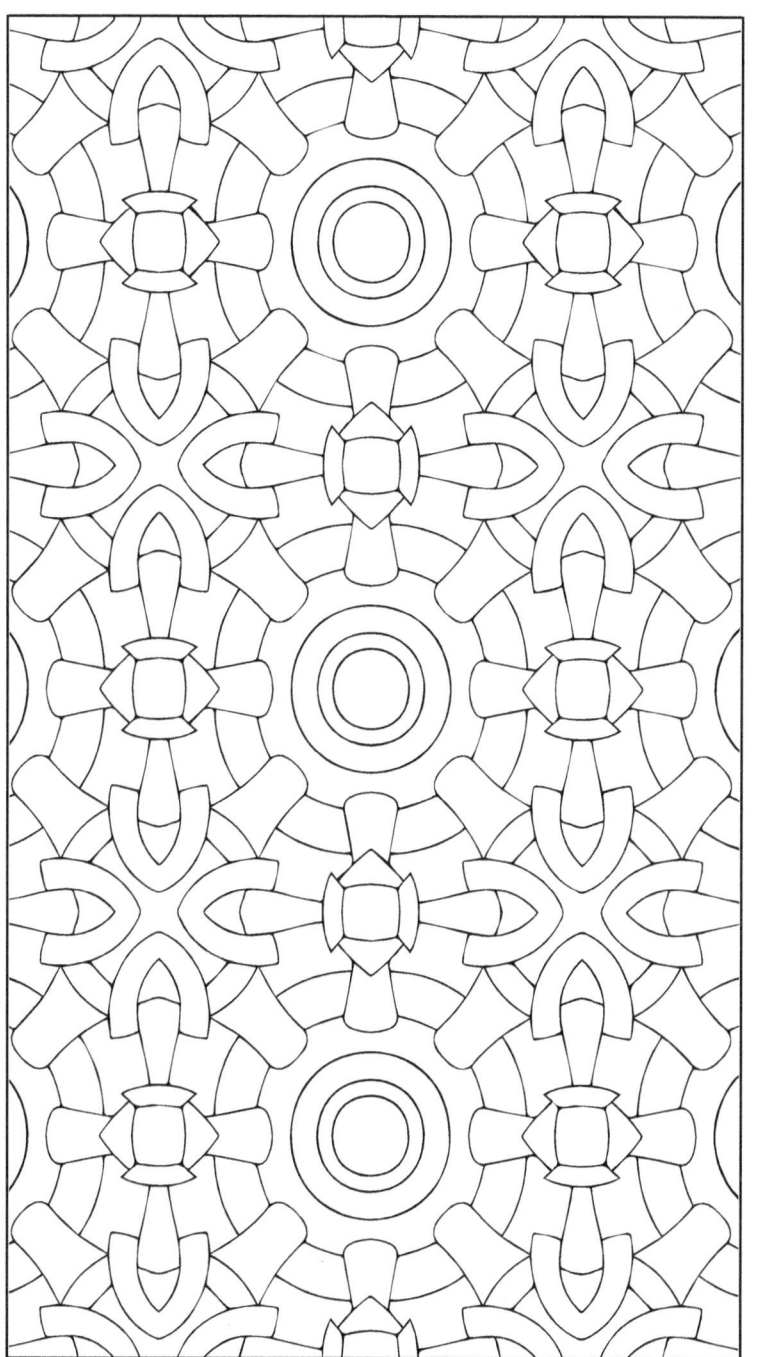

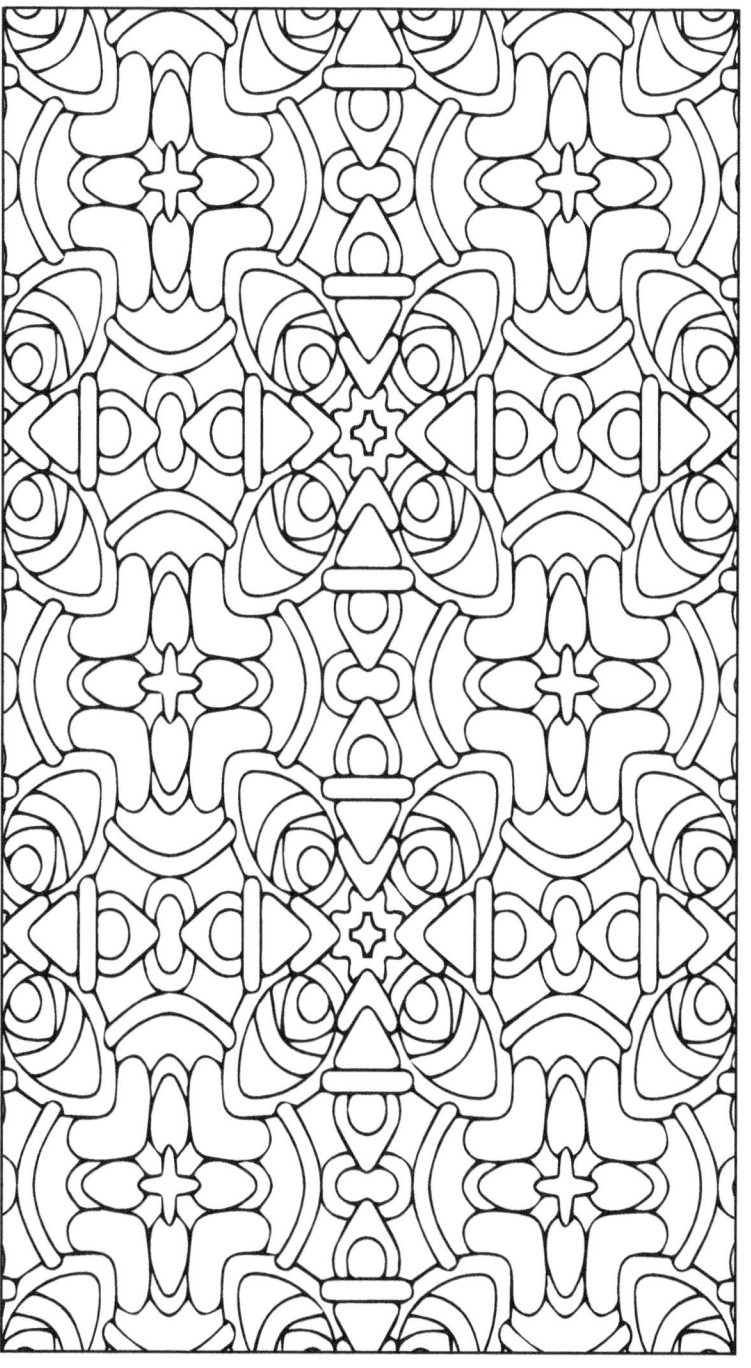

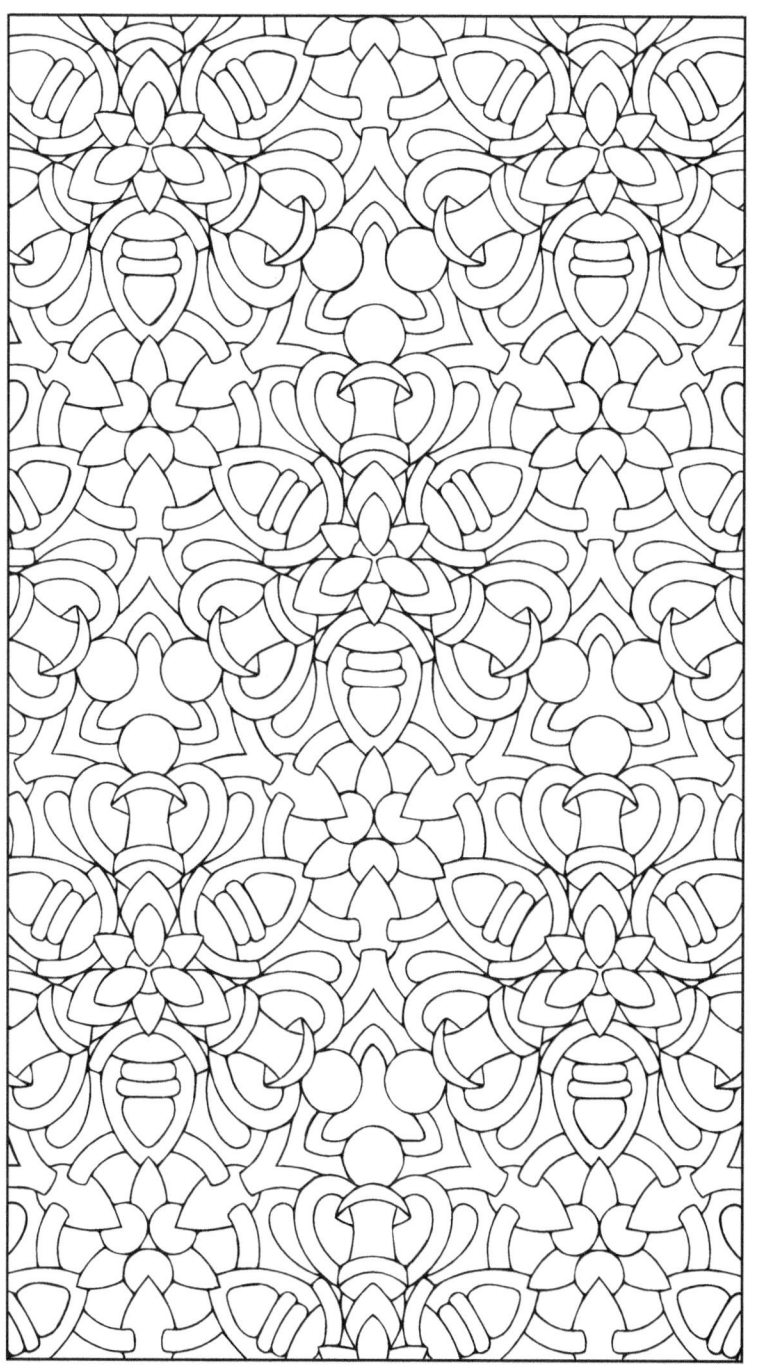

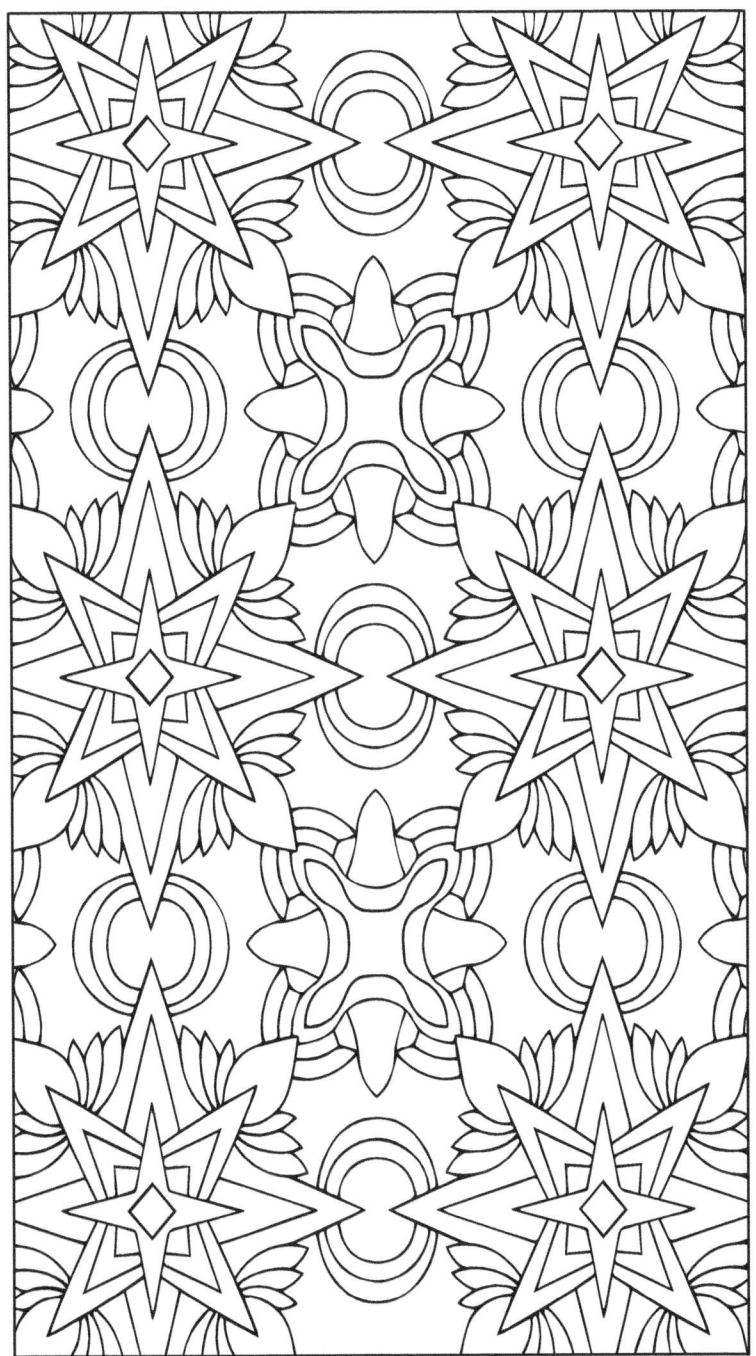

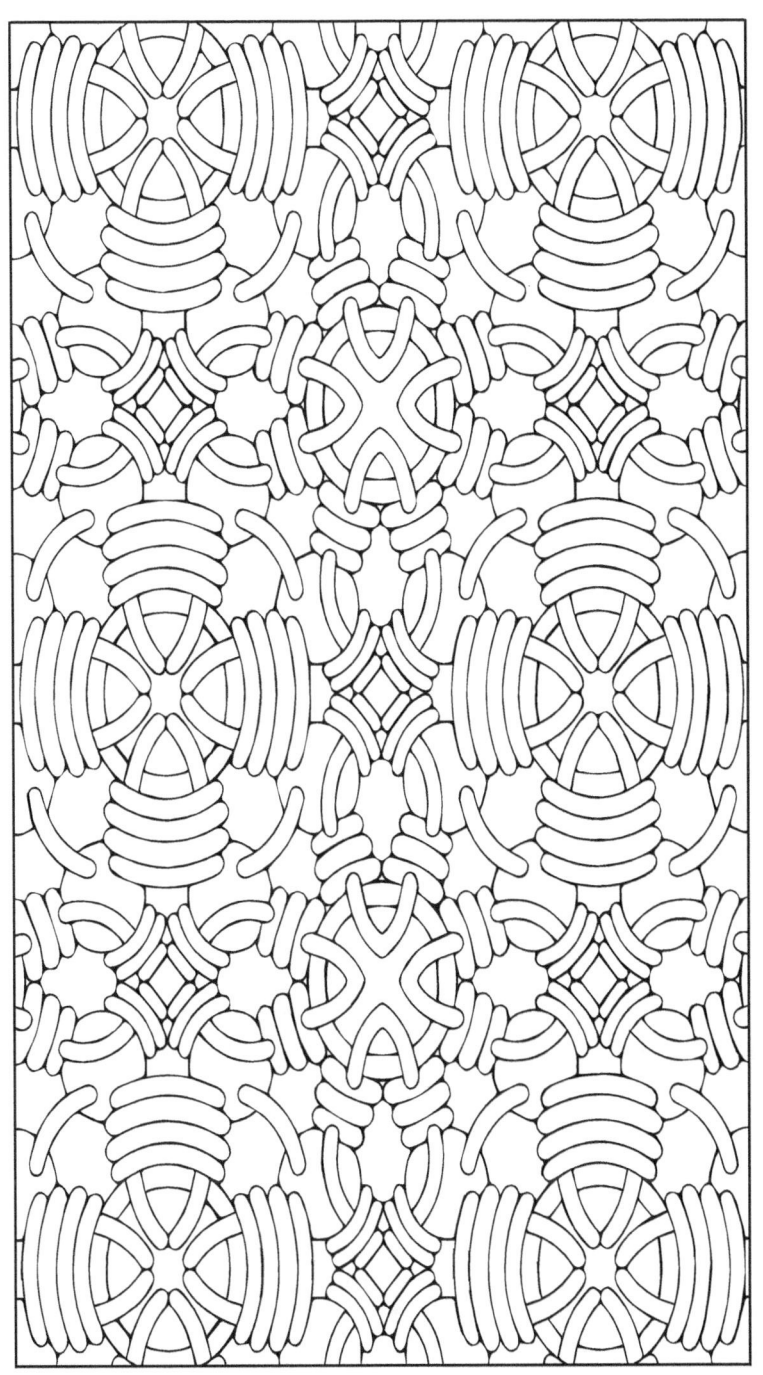

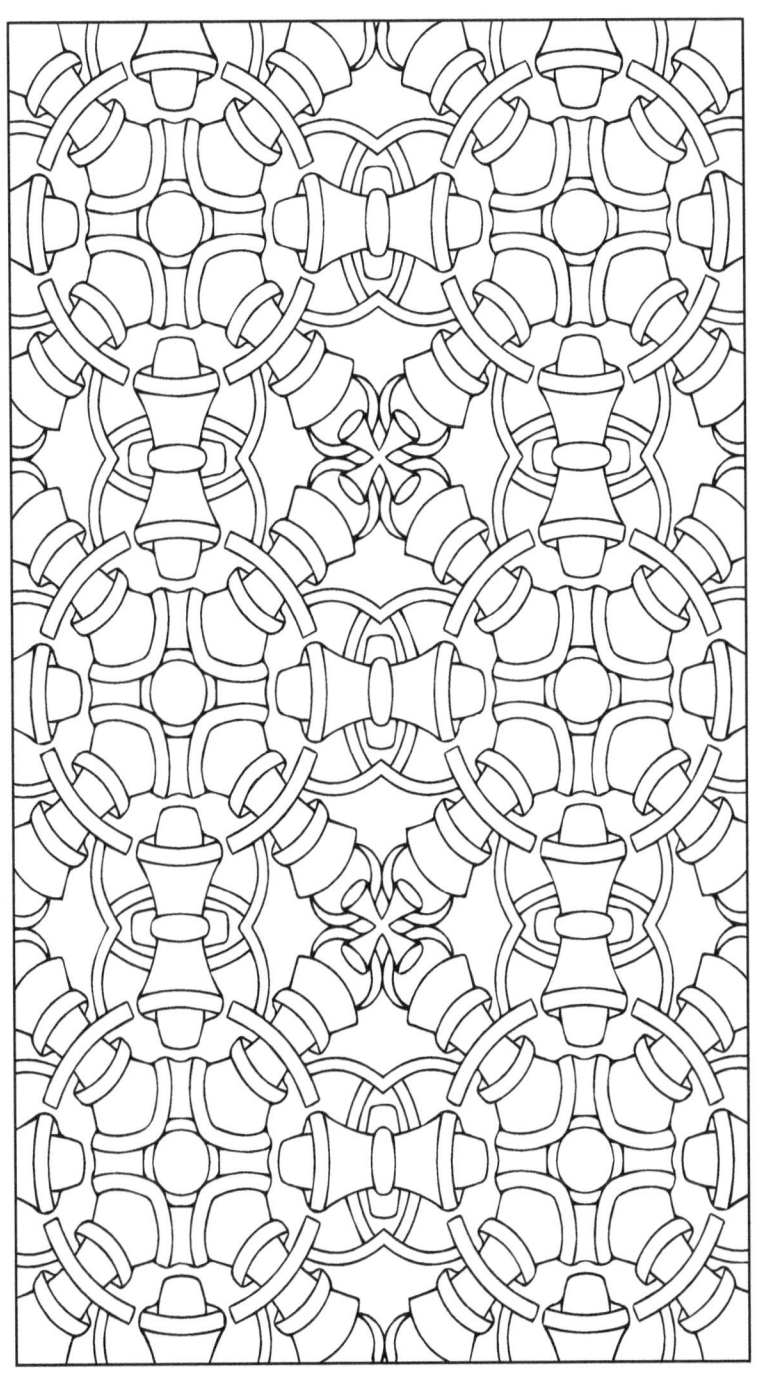

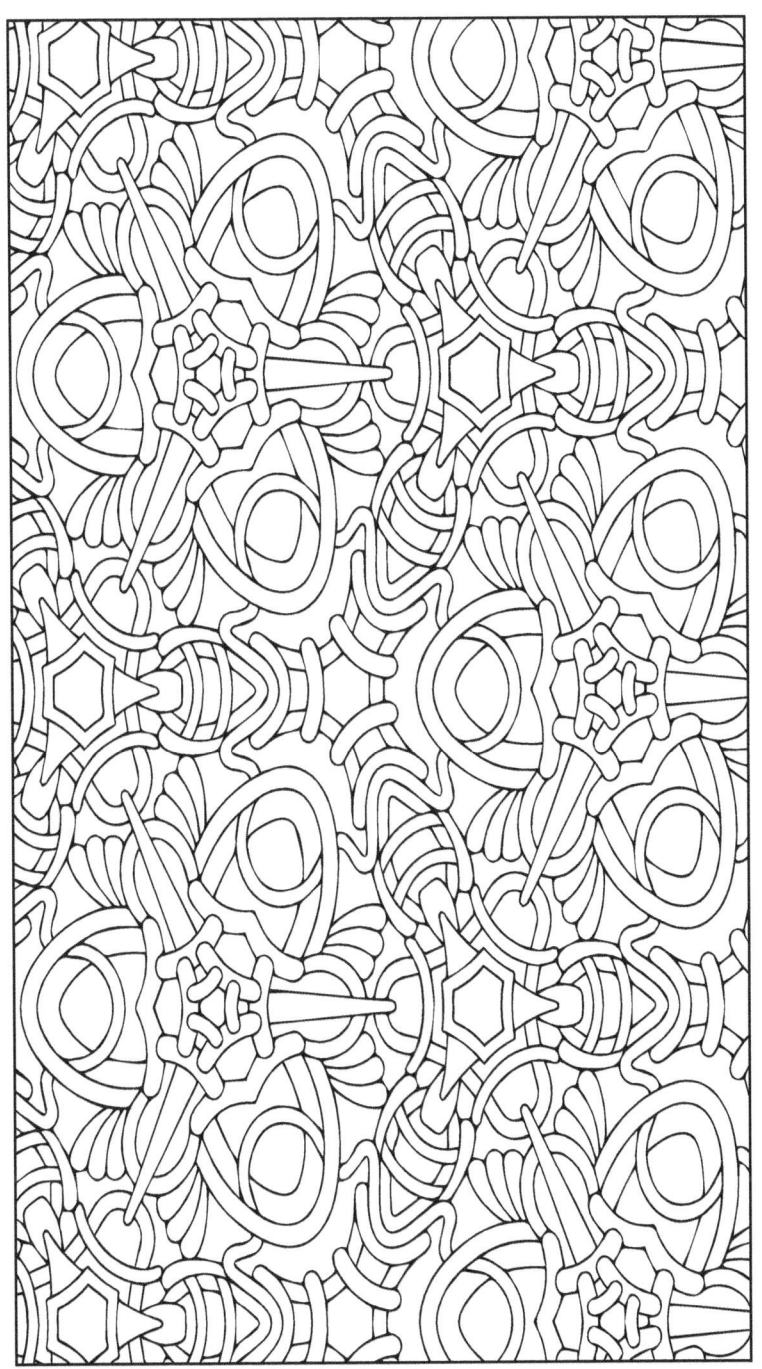

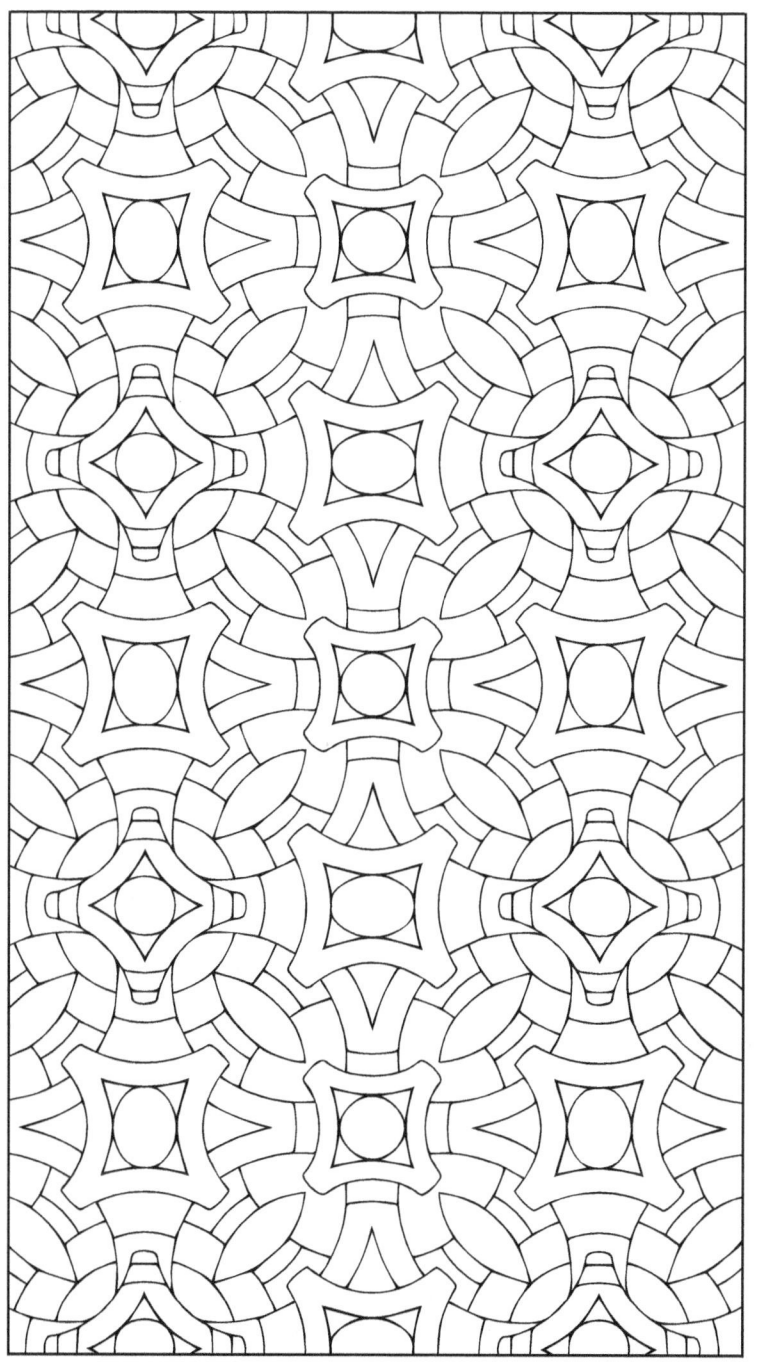

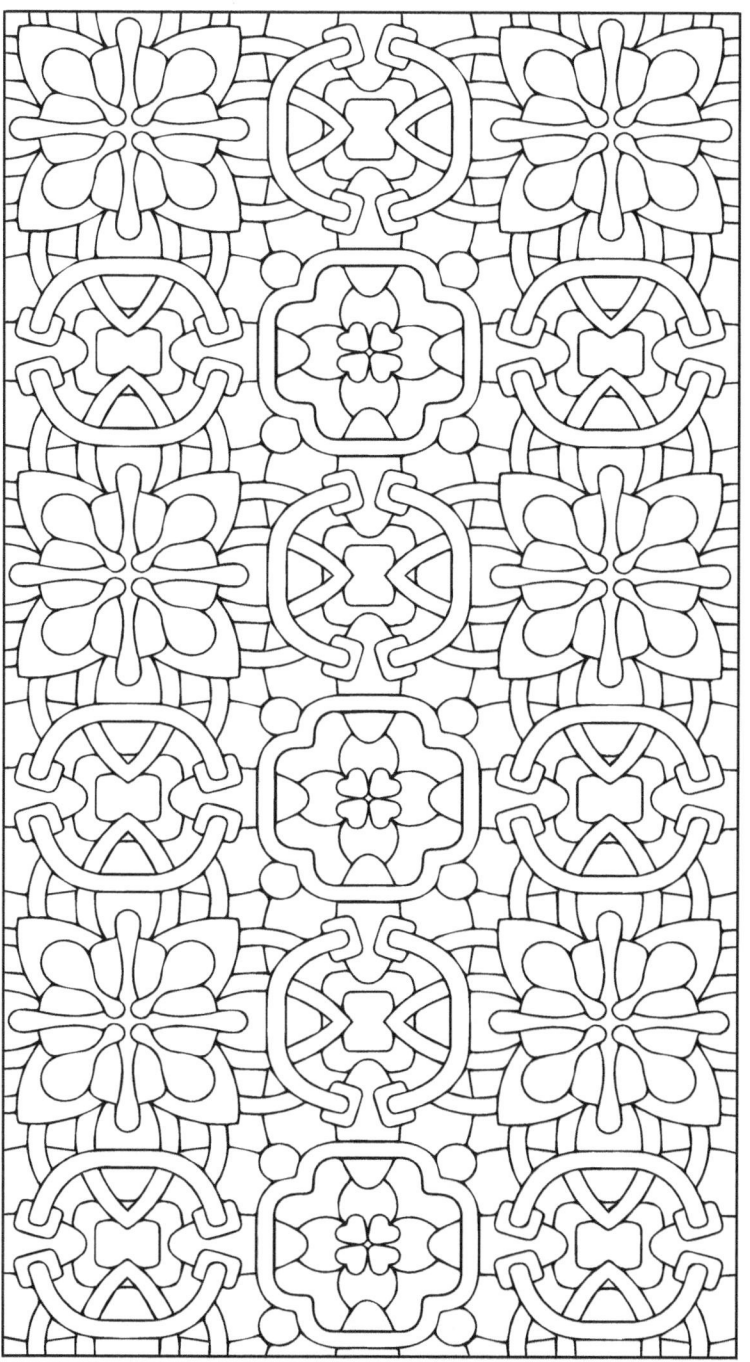

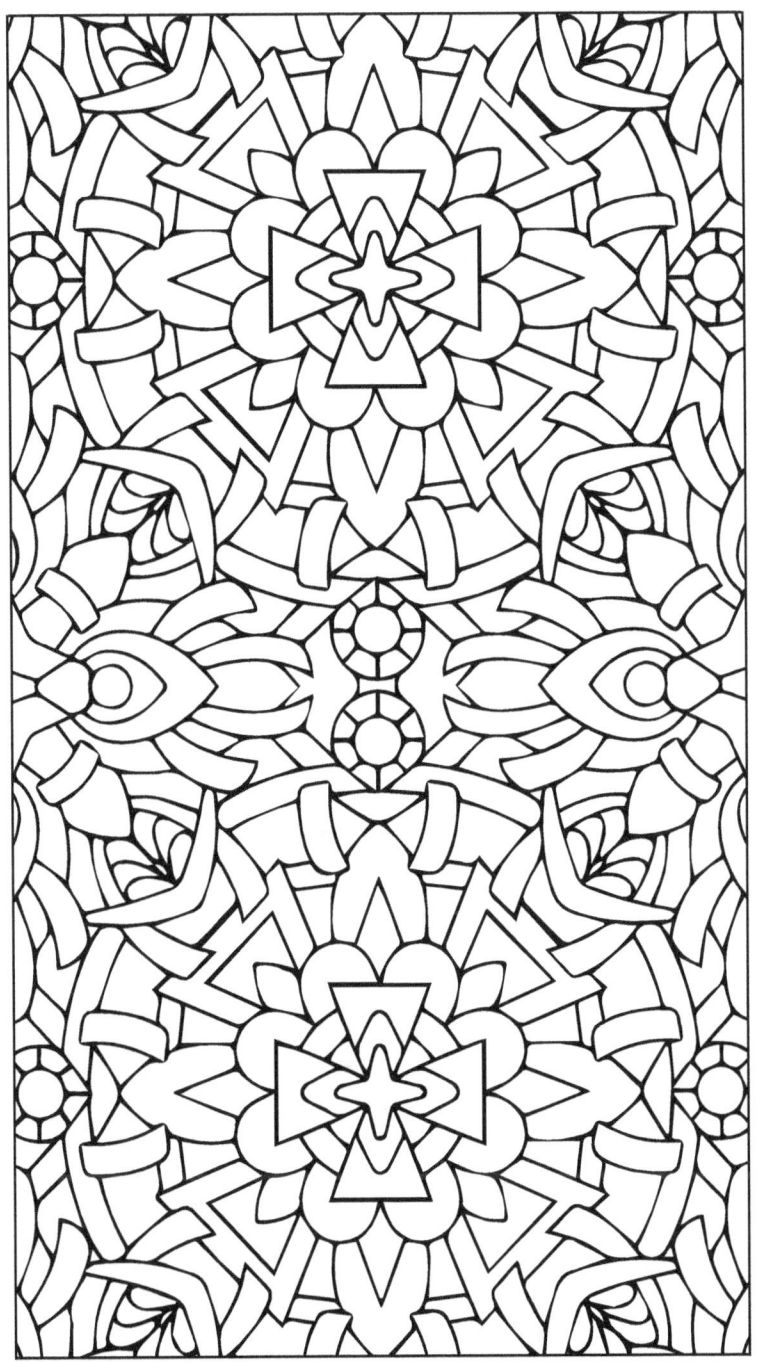

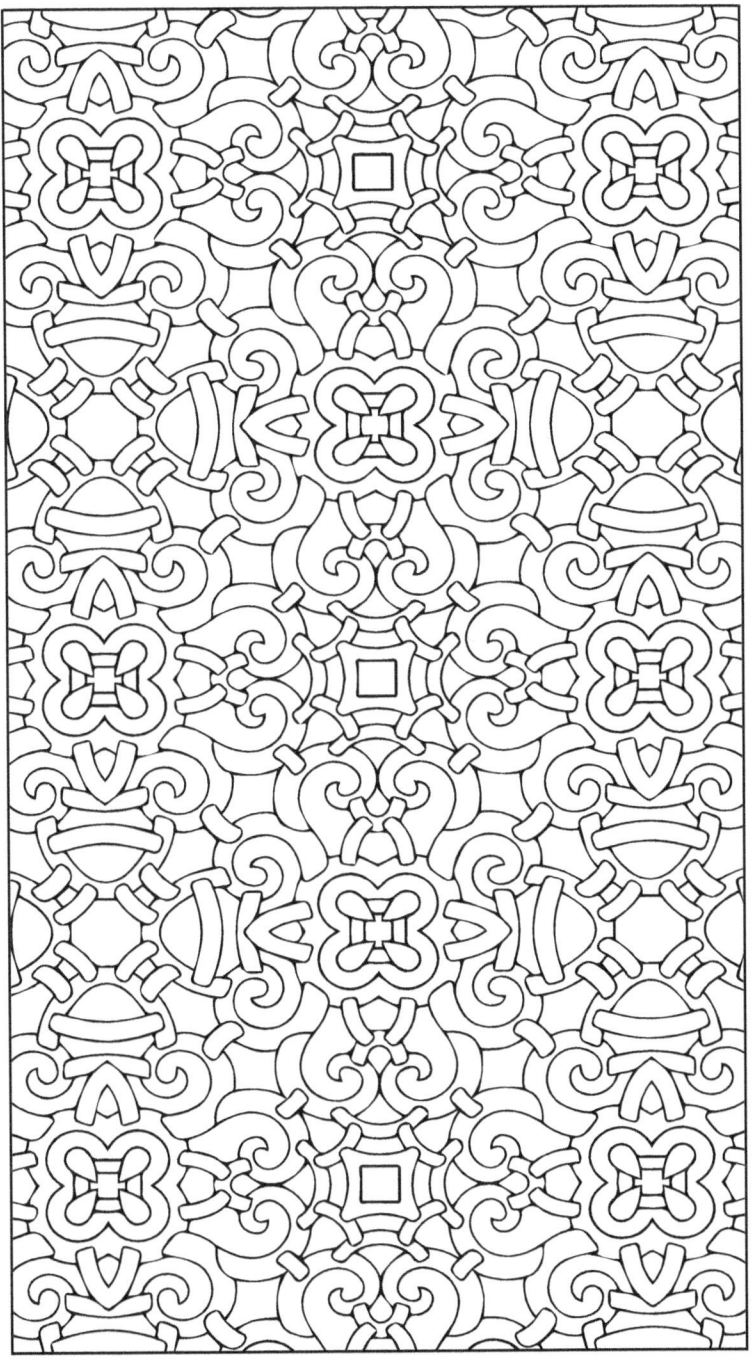

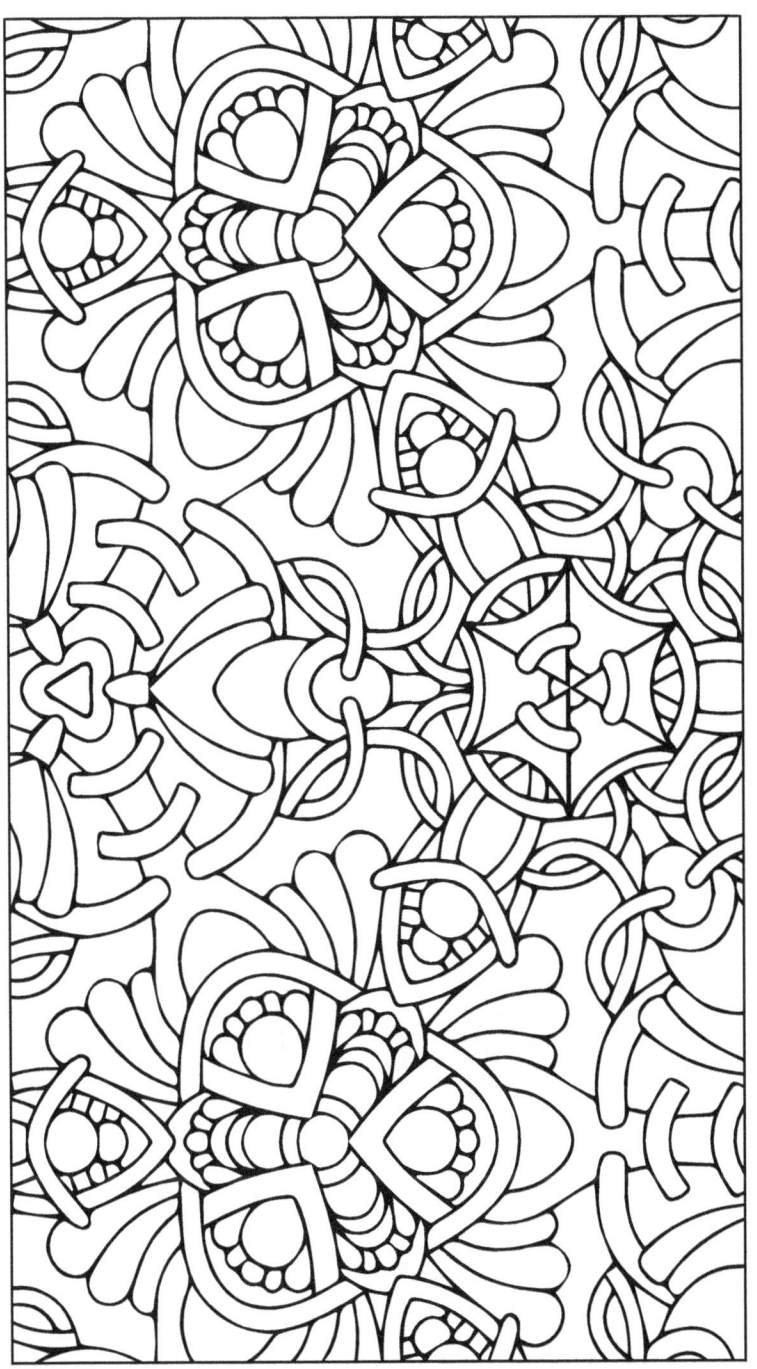

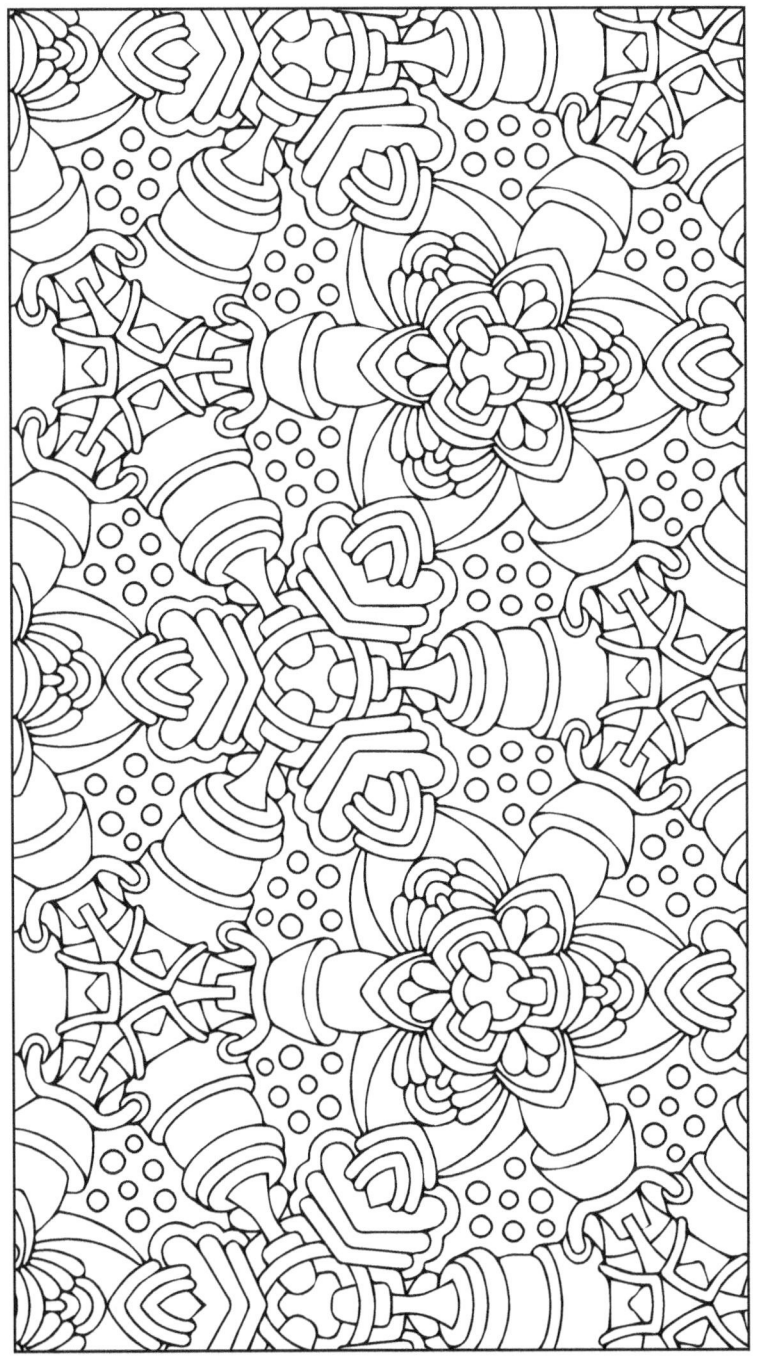

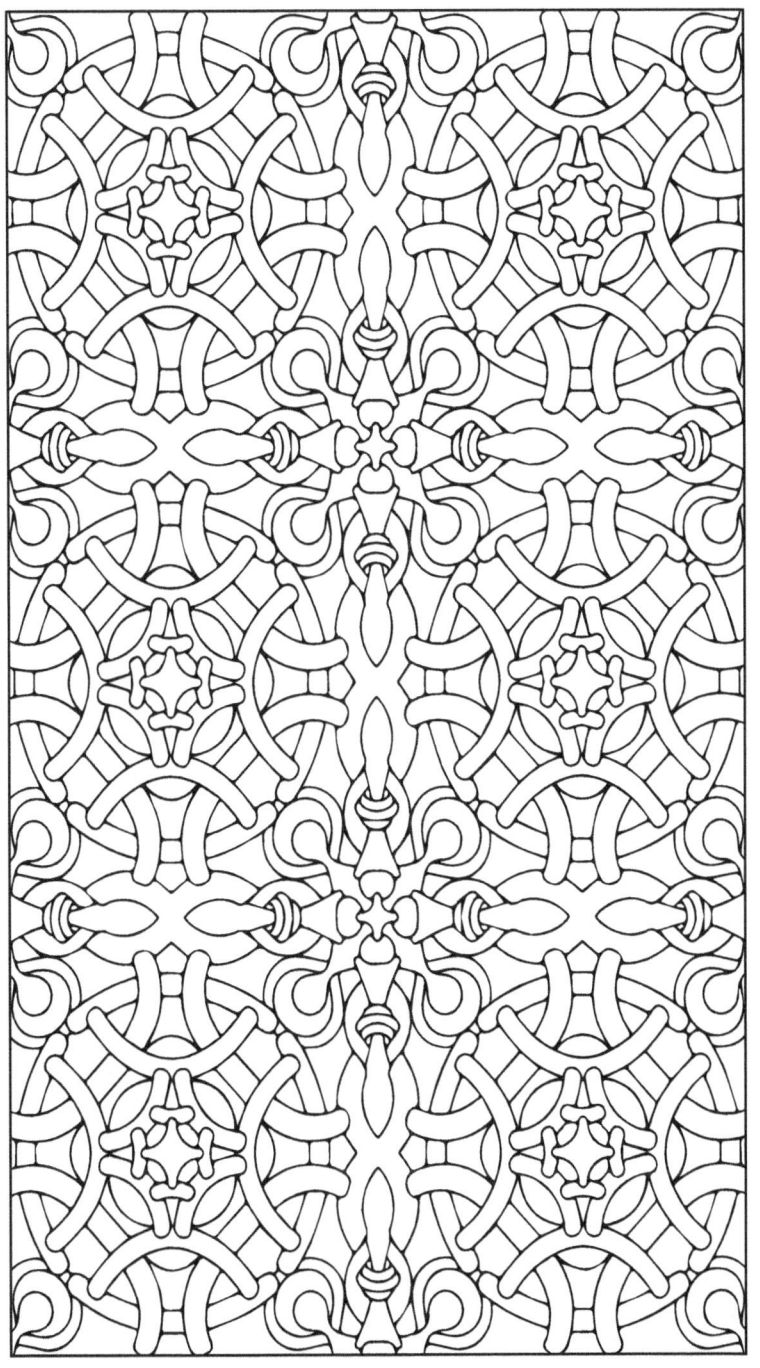

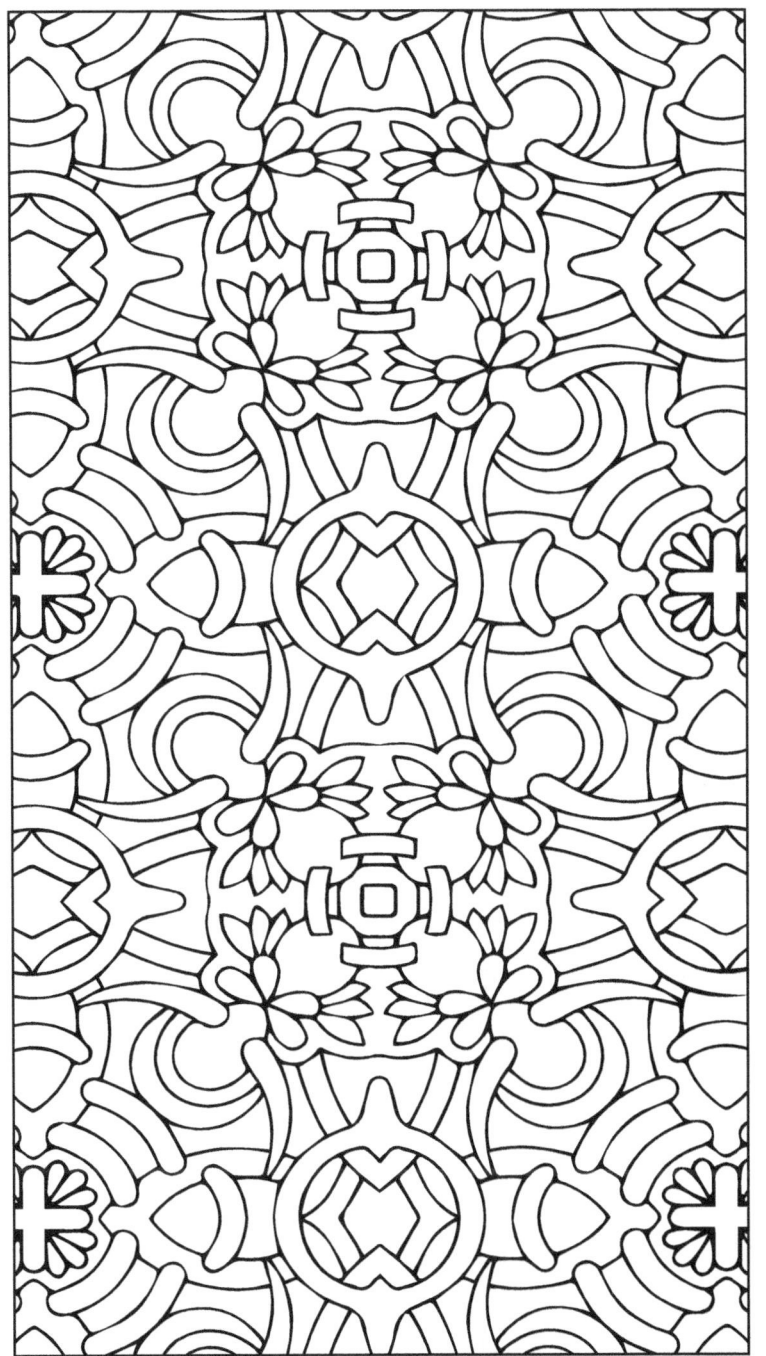

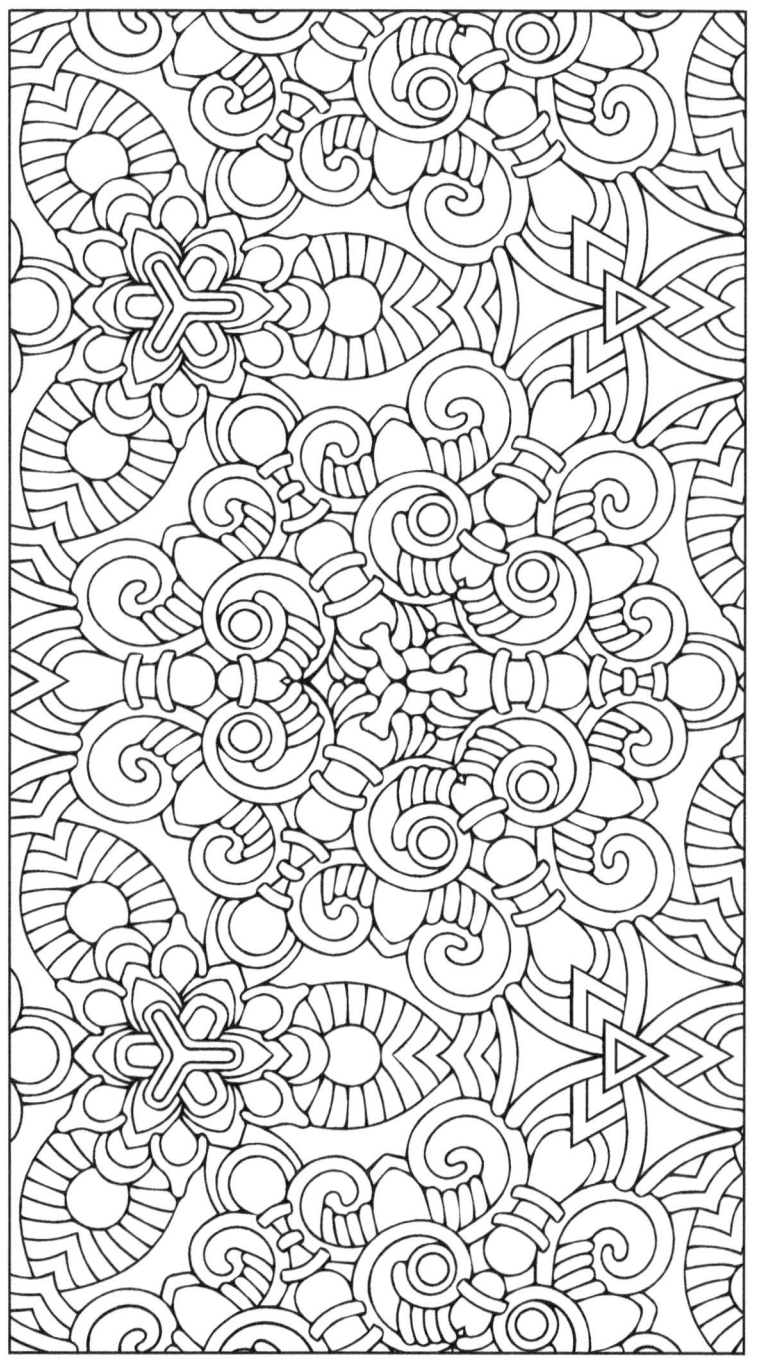

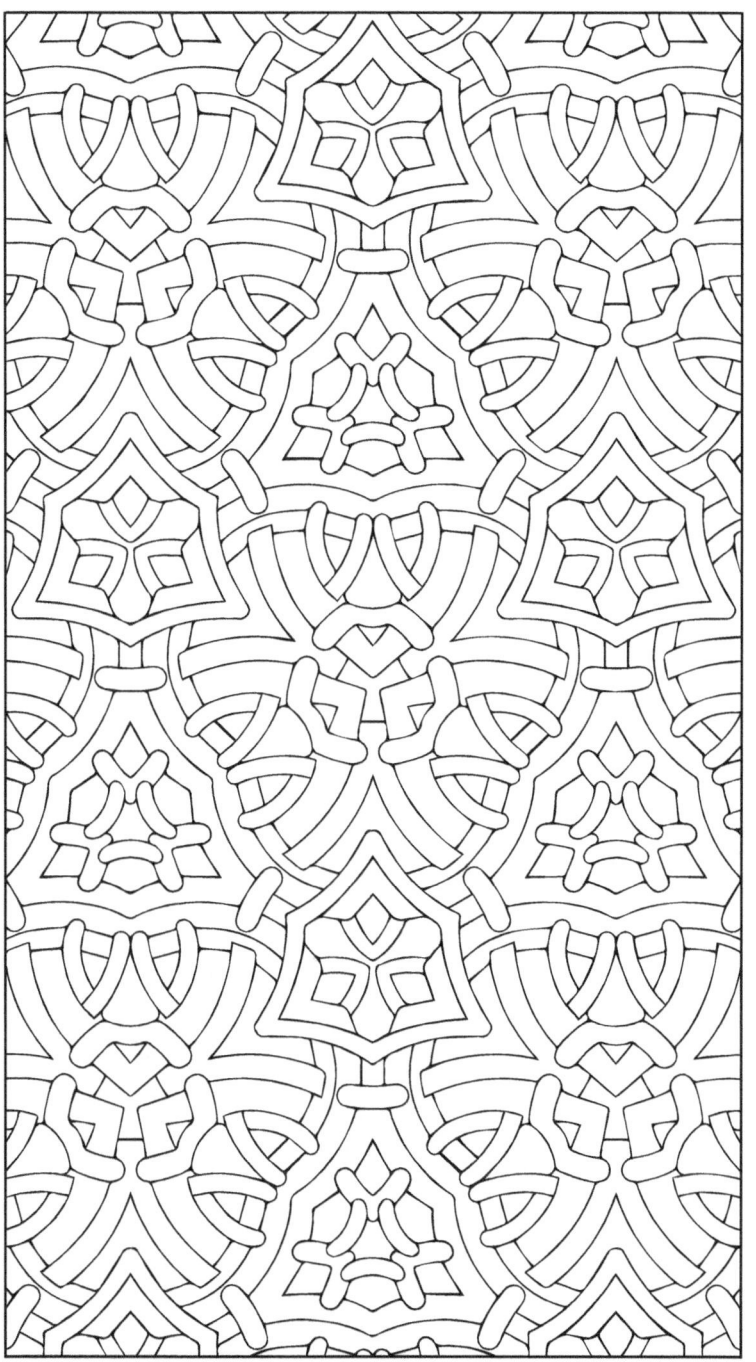

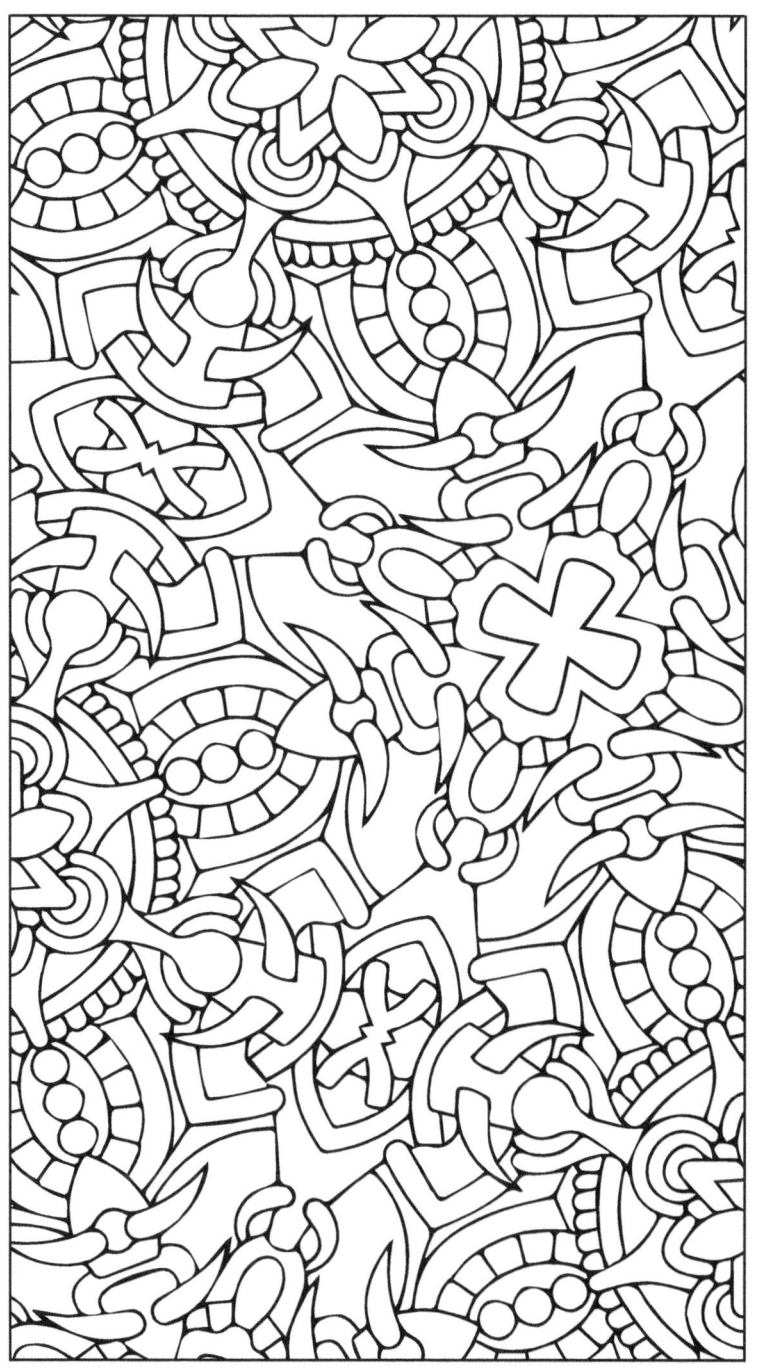

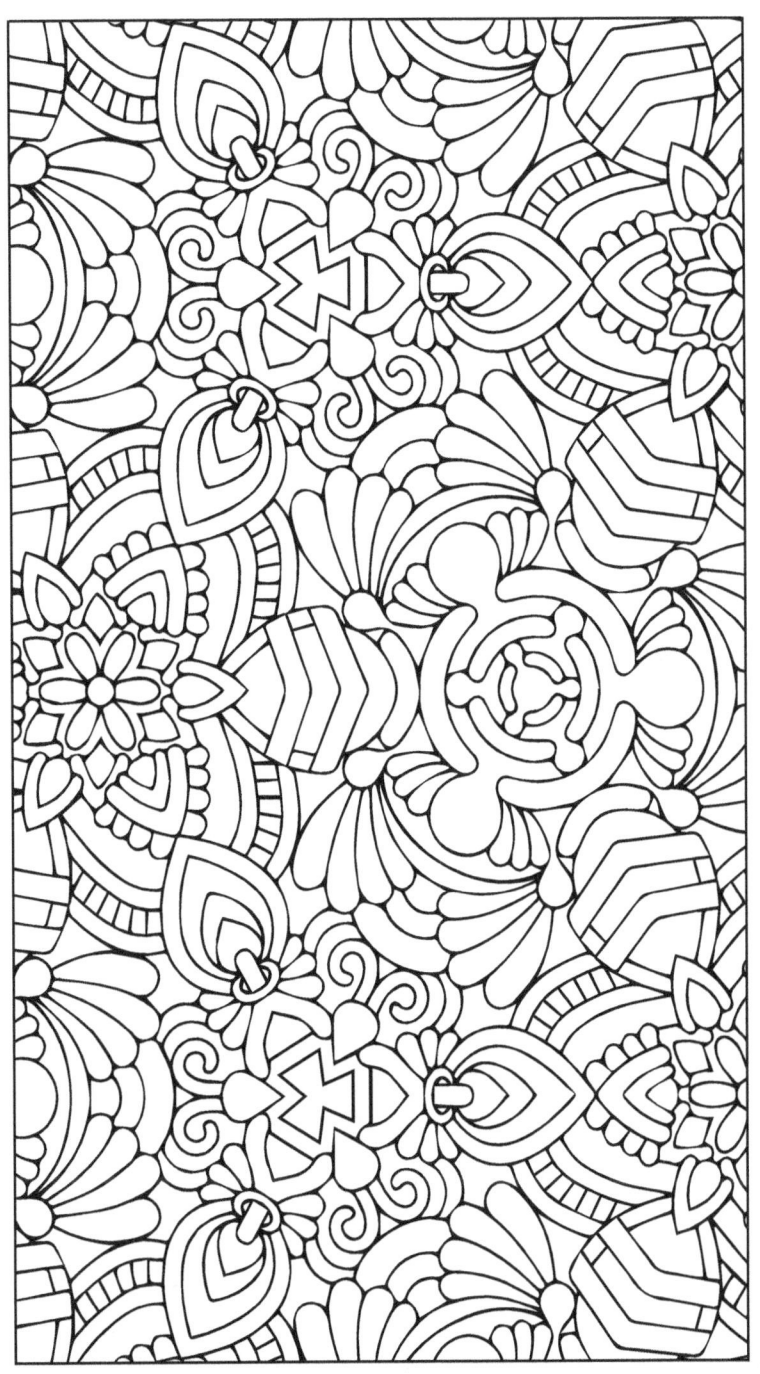

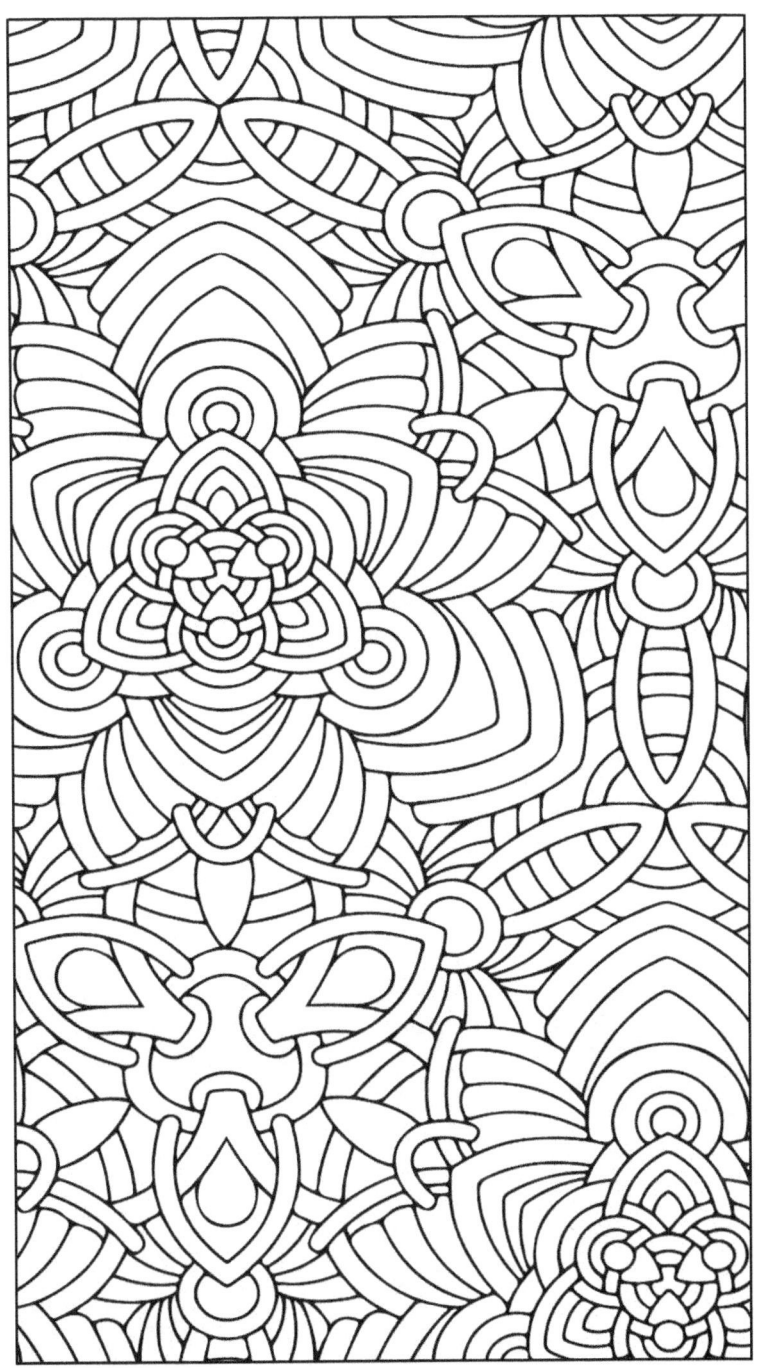

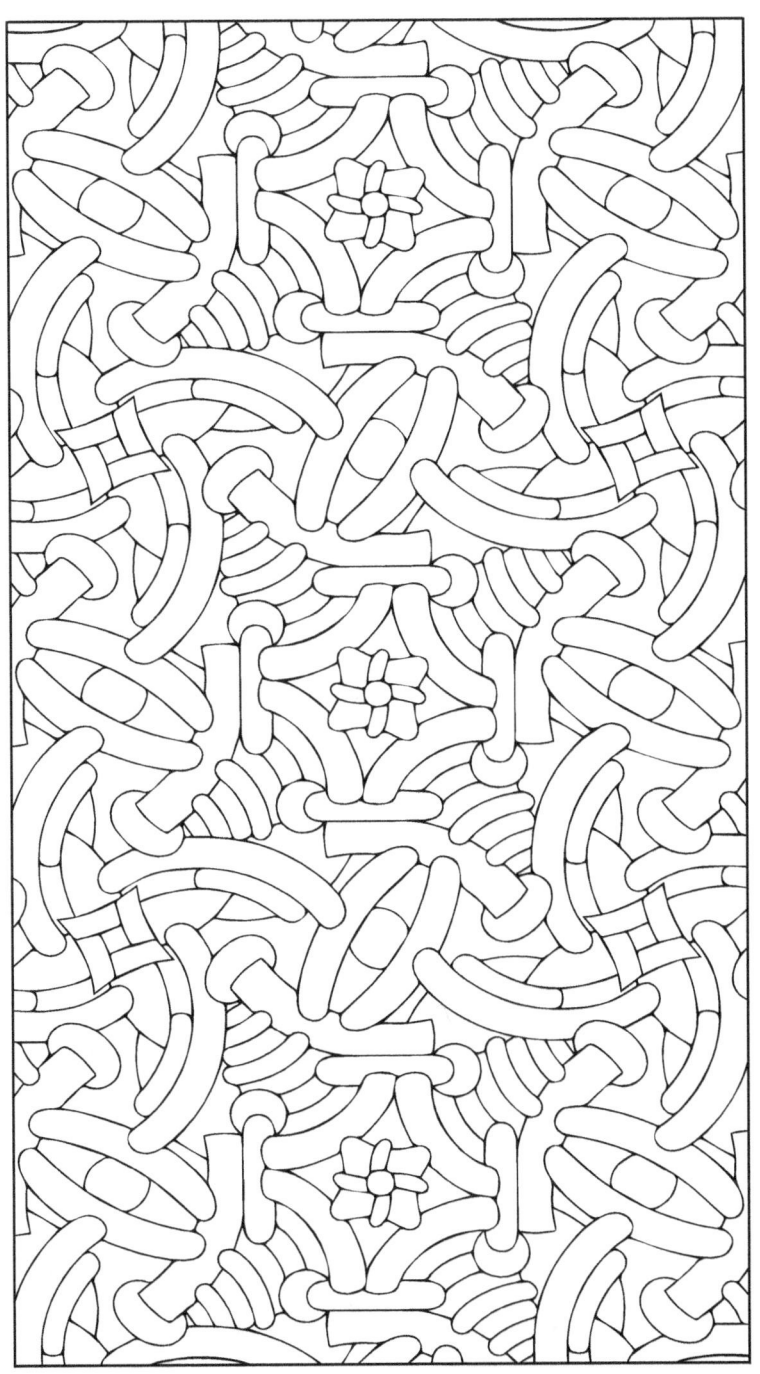

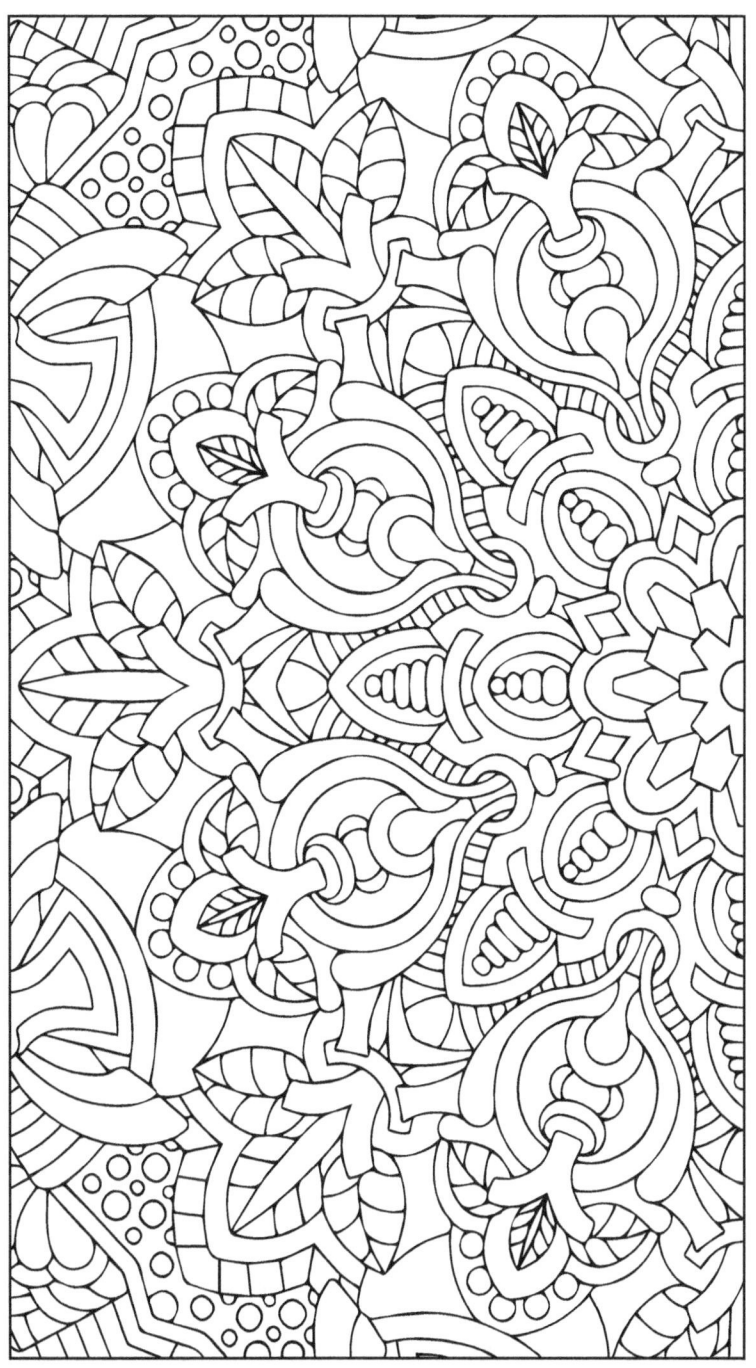

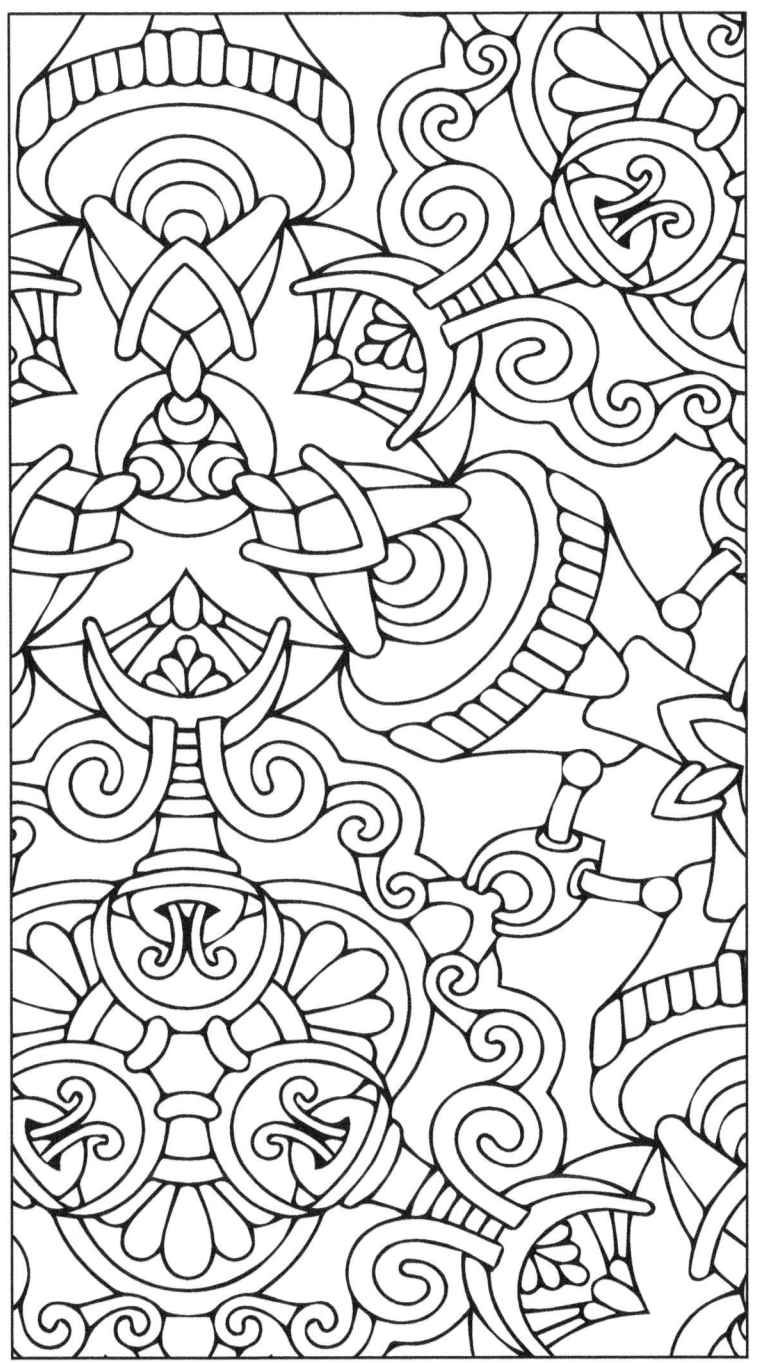

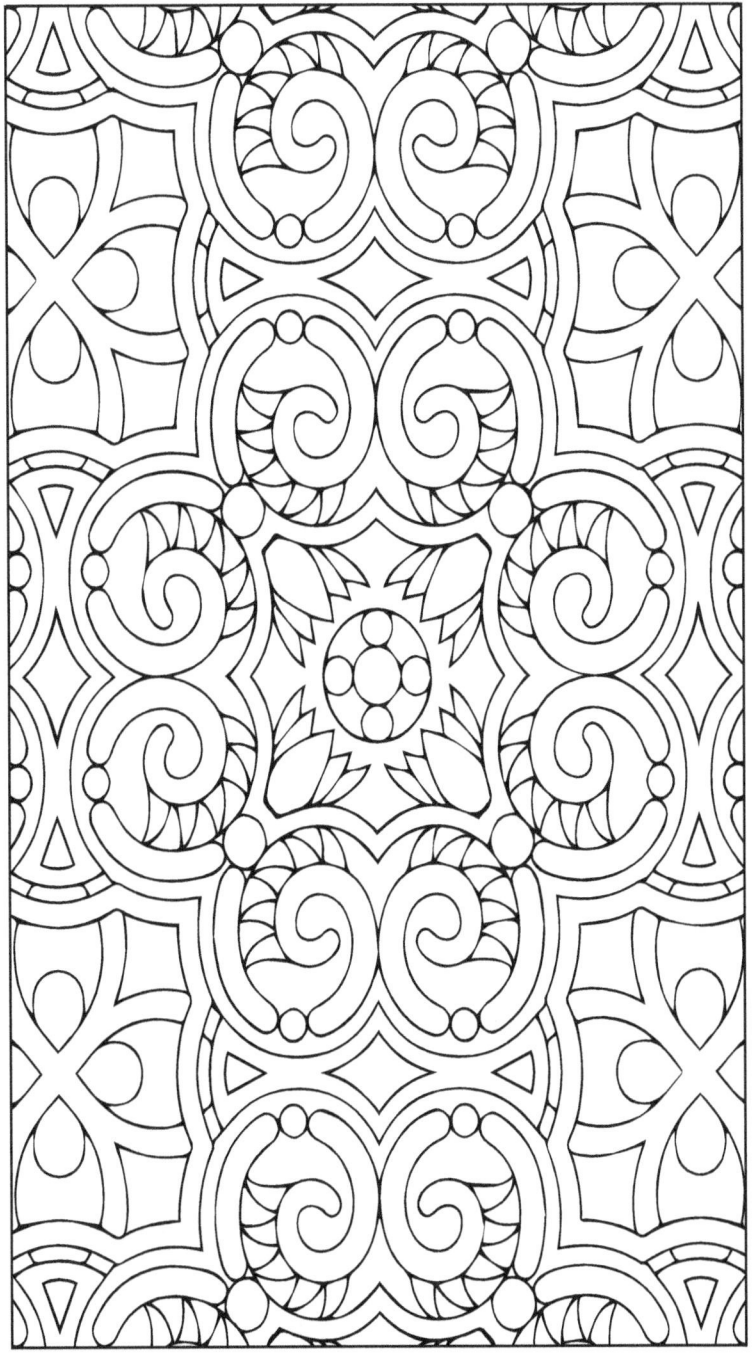

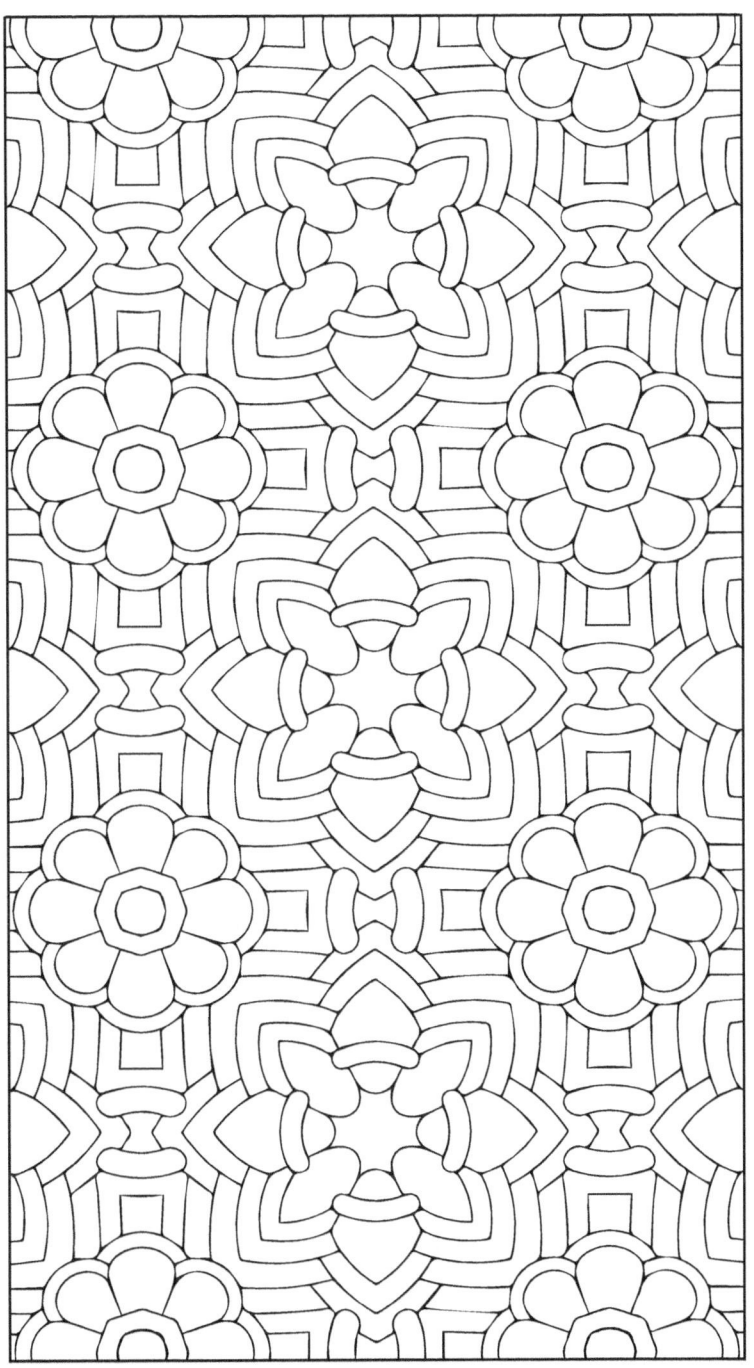

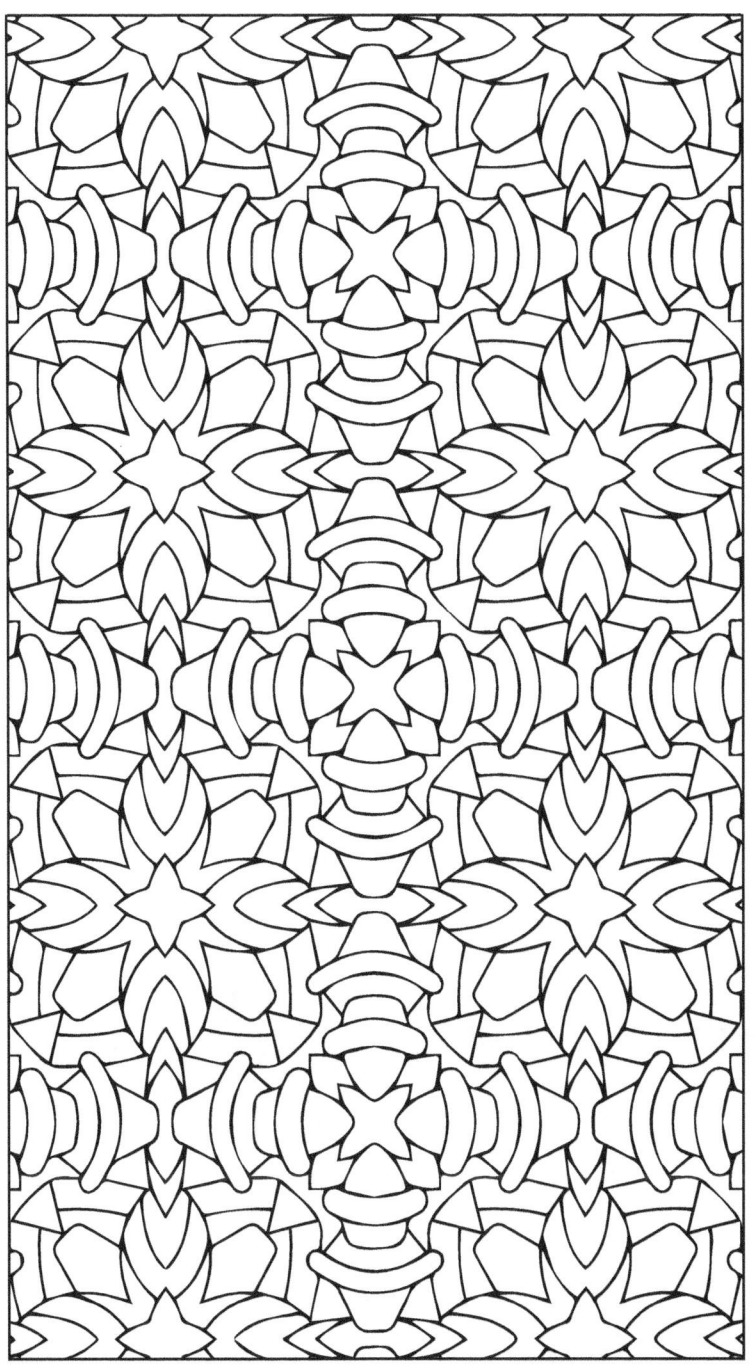

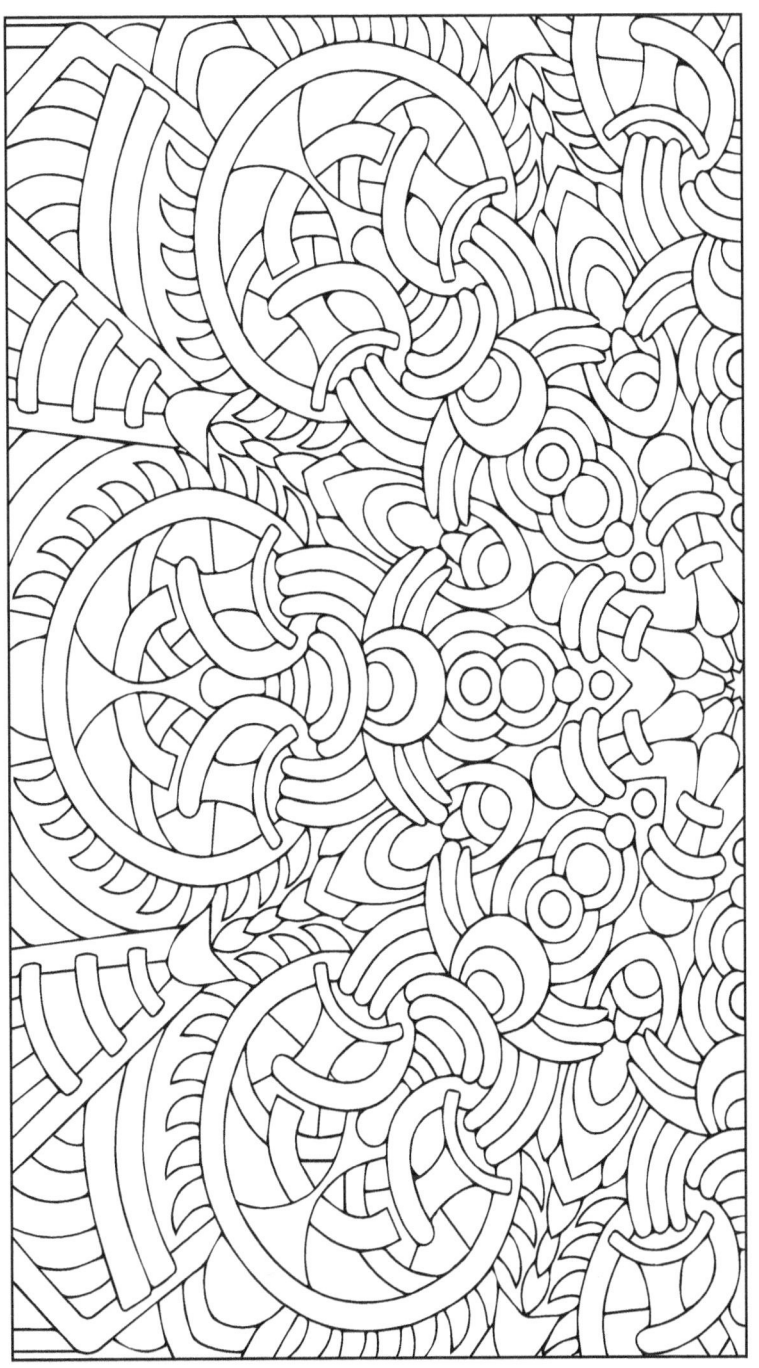

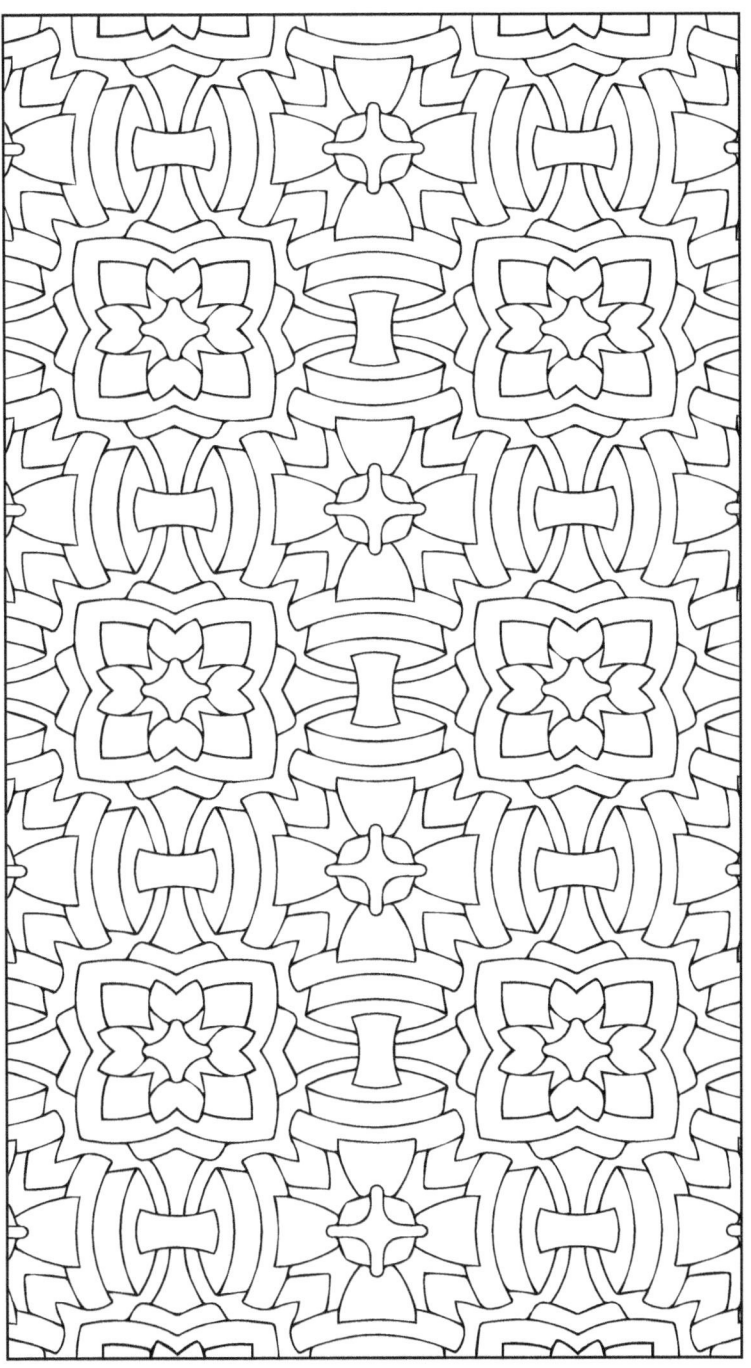

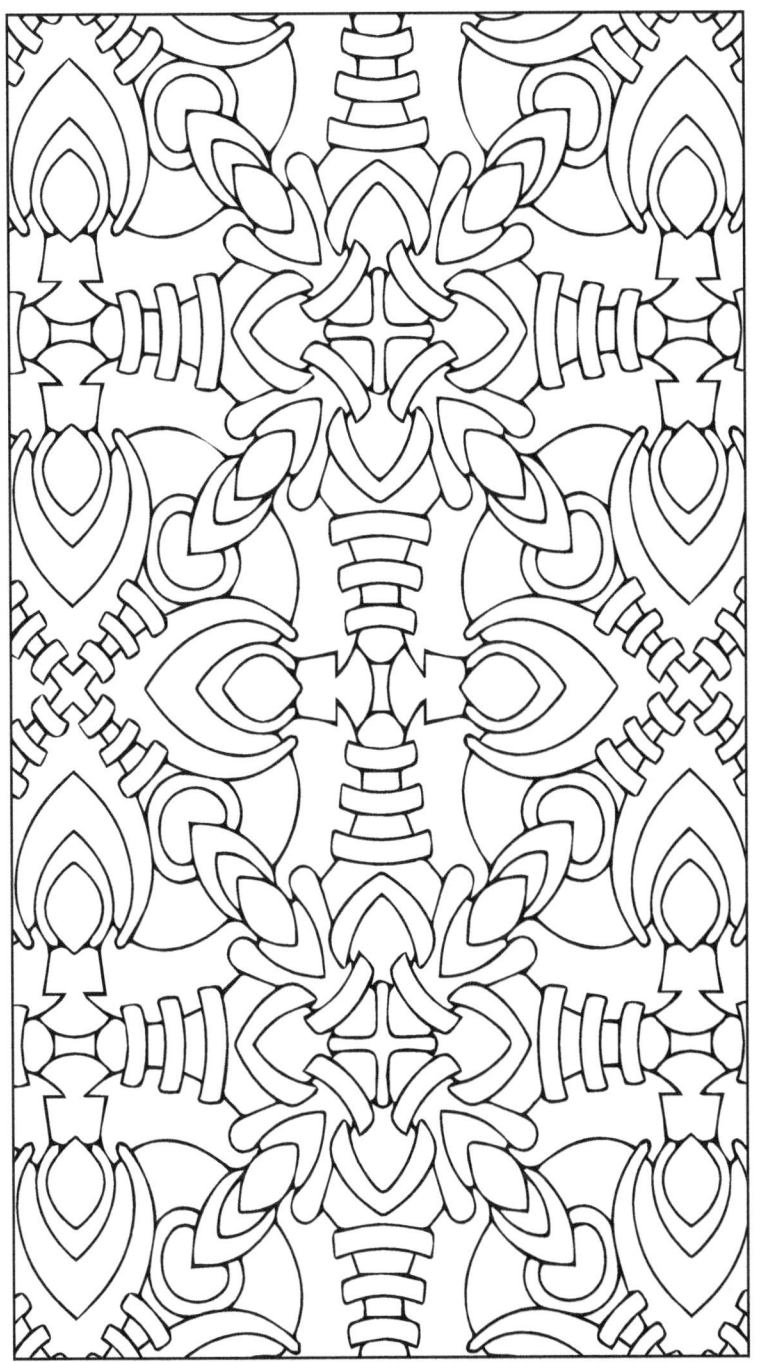

Also by Lori Greenberg

Mandala Coloring Books
Meditative Mandalas - Volume 1
Relaxing Mandalas - Volume 2
Calming Mandalas - Volume 3
Fanciful Mandalas - Volume 4

Pattern Coloring Books
Meditative Patterns - Volume 1
Relaxing Patterns - Volume 2
Calming Patterns - Volume 3
Pocket Patterns - Volume 1

Affirmation Coloring Books
Meditative Affirmations - Volume 1

Find these, and future books on Amazon

Visit **www.lorigreenberg.com**
and join Lori Greenberg's Coloring
Connection Facebook group
for free coloring pages
and updates on new books.

www.ingramcontent.com/pod-product-compliance
Lightning Source LLC
Chambersburg PA
CBHW071235170526
45165CB00003B/1099